LIFE'S A SALES CALL

How to Succeed in the World's Oldest Profession

SECOND EDITION

By Jack Warkenthien

Updated and with a Foreword by Juanell Teague

LIFE'S A SALES CALL

How to Succeed in the World's Oldest Profession

By Jack Warkenthien

©Copyright 2015

SECOND EDITION

NSS PRESS

Published by NSS Press
5090 Richmond Ave. Suite 400
Houston TX 77056
www.nextstep-solutions.com

Printed in the United States of America

ISBN 978-0-9752737-2-2 $19.95

Cover & Interior design by Kemi Kim

Foreword by Juanell Teague

To say the world of selling has changed is an understatement. Gone forever are the days of clever, pre-rehearsed closes, canned responses to customer objections and waiting without listening while the prospect speaks so you can give the next sales point. Sales is no longer a prepackaged presentation, delivered to prospects without understanding their individual wants and needs.

I used to be a part of that world; I thought that was the way to sell; and, at the time it was acceptable behavior.

Today buyers are more knowledgeable, confident, discerning and skeptical. The internet has enabled the consumer to find more information than ever before, to know when a sales men is on target and when they are clueless.

Yet , the fundamental need to have others buy from you continues today as always. We may need to change our attitudes and approaches, but the bottom line remains the bottom line.

Jack understand the bottom line. And he understands this transformation in the sales arena. When I first encountered Jack, it was from his reputation. I had left my career promoting speaker rallies and had entered the world of consulting, working with speakers to help them deepen, position and market their careers. Jack was coming into the speaking industry in San Antonio and was working with major insurance companies then. He had a great story.

He's been big at IBM. During his decade-long career with IBM, he led the nation in new account sales. He had quickly established a stellar reputation as a team leader, and earned their highest sales award of EAGLE, his second year on quota. As I learned about Jack, I developed a deep respect for his goal setting, determination and success in sales at IBM.

Jack is an excellent student. When I worked with Jack, I was amazed at his dedication. Every task we identified he jumped on. He didn't just complete the task, he completed it with determination, energy and speed. He wasted no time pondering the problems or debating the difficulties. He just did it.

I also got to know Jack on a personal level. From our conversations I know he is a dedicated father and husband. He loves and respects his wife and supports her in her own business. He loves his children and places them at a cornerstone in his life, continually focusing on his teaching and role modeling.

As we have stayed in touch through the years, have watched Jack continue to grow and develop his theory. And I've watched him mellow. Success at IBM requires an ego. IBM looks for it, hires it and promotes it.

Since leaving IBM, Jack has retained all of his self- confidence, but he's sanded the edges of the ego. He is still a high-energy, non-stop, make-it-happen guy. But he's also let his natural servant heart, caring leadership and encouraging spirit show through more than IBM might have let it.

Jack's new book, Life's a Sales Call, captures his story. It provides both the information and the inspiration to enable others to succeed as he has. More than a simple tutorial, or a recipe, his book weaves the story with the content. It isn't just a good read, it's a fun read too.

As I read the book, I remembered our initial work and our conversations through the years. I remembered Jack's presentation at one of my client conferences. I remembered Jack's accomplishments, strengths and successes. But the part of the book that meant the most to me was that Jack shared his vulnerabilities, his setbacks and his failures. It takes great strength to open up and share this personal side of life with others. Most authors of "business success" books won't do that.

Jack did.

Jack's book is different for this reason. Jack is a hope merchant. He helps others to see, not just that their success is possible, but that he has been where they were, stumbled as they have and not always taken the direct road. Jack's book exposes the bare bones truth. It is real. It is authentic. It is Jack.

Dedication

January 20, 1954 - March 11, 2005

Life's A Sales Call! Nobody "lived" that premise more
completely than my good friend, Frank LaFemina. I dedicate this
book to Frank who passed all too soon.   My only regret is that I
didn't meet him decades earlier in life.

Frank La Femina, who leaves his wife Judy and stepson Brent
Ford worked hard and played hard. He left nothing on the table
at the end of the day. Whether it was "opening" relationships as
the AFLAC State Sales Coordinator, or hunting hogs in
Pleasanton, Texas, Frank was fond of saying "Let's get 'er done,"
and he always did, with passion, enthusiasm and class.

I thank my dear friend, John Matthews, for bringing us together.
John Matthews started out as a client, but quickly became a
confidante, friend and go-to person whenever we needed
something. Frank, John and I were known as the "three amigos"
for an all too short period of time.

Frank, this book's for you! Save us a place in your foursome.
We'll catch you on the turn!

v

Acknowledgments

In the Fall of 1975, I started my second year at the University of Illinois, in Champaign-Urbana. As a Delta Sigma Phi, I was responsible for perpetuating our good name on campus, by "rushing" future Delta Sigs.

Almost forty years later to the day, as I complete the revision of this book, I realize that the fraternity "sales" experience was the beginning of my sales career. My job was to "sell" students on joining our House. I was good at it -didn't know why at the time -but I was very effective. Now, with the completion of this labor of love, I share the secret "sauce," the recipe, for all to savor.

Writing a bestseller is absolutely a team sport. The "captain" of our team was Laura Baker, my writing coach, editor and the person who kept me "on point" for a project that was five years in the making. I'm quite certain that without Laura, this project would still be a vision without a plan - or worse - a hallucination! You're the best, Laura!

Professionally speaking, my first partner and longtime friend, Tony Diamond, co-founder of Diamond Warkenthien Associates (precursor to NextStep Solutions) was an inspiration twenty years ago. He encouraged me to write one of the best sales training platforms ever. Thanks, Tony!

Another marquee player was Juanell Teague, founder of People Plus. She made me "Focus or Die," uncovering my life's turning points. Thanks for helping me discover the brilliance within - and for writing your heartfelt foreword.

With a supporting cast too numerous to name, I'm going to try my best: Jim Eskin, Jeffrey Gitomer, Jon "Spike" Erwin, Diane Simpson, Rick Banta, Mark Victor Hansen, Jack Canfield, Roy Williams (The Wizard of Ads), Morris Miller and others who encouraged me to write this book.

Linda Elliott has inspired me for as long as I've known her. She's the best networker I've ever met. Today, she makes a living sharing her "connection" skills with the world. She was also my very first radio guest. Linda, thanks for including me in your "Elliott Connection."

My sister Luann (a.k.a. Sis!) is always there for me when I need a sister's opinion. She's so well-grounded and great to have as a sounding board. I love her dearly. Luann, is that a ship I see in the harbor. ...?

Dad (Reinhardt Warkenthien) continues to be the benchmark and role model for how I'd like to be, as a father to our teenage boys. The most unselfish and giving man I've ever met -and brilliant at being a competent Mr. Fix-it. I'll never outgrow my "Daddy- do" lists - and Dad will never see the end of 'em!

Then there's Ma. My mom, Pauline, was definitely the sales pro in our family. I thank her for all the communication and relationship gifts that she passed on to me. She's still the best salesperson I've ever met, and I learn from her every time we chat. Since she's never met a stranger, she's fun to network with as well. Ma, the apple doesn't fall far from the tree!

Sons Nick, Ross and Will who are carving their own paths in life, traversing three different States, are the epitome of millennials. All are salesmen in their own way, though none sell for a living.

They continue to challenge me--in their own signature style-- though mostly via telephone calls, that is, if I can convince them to make the call, instead of using the "handier" text function.

Now, let me introduce you to the reason for this "season": Kemi Kim, my inspiration and Wife. She is not just made in Korea, she's Royalty, descendent of the last King, KyungSoon of the Shila Dynasty-- and we were made FOR each other-- at this stage of our life. In fact, it was Kemi's idea to rewrite this book, and her persistence as the editor of this updated version of Life's A Sales Call. Her favorite mantra is, "I'm not in Sales", though she's one of the best persuaders I've ever met. Heck, I was ready to pen a totally different book this year, to keep my modest streak intact (to author one book every five years), and look at me now! Kemi knows me better than anyone, outside my birth family, and isn't that what defines a great Sales person- -know your "customer" intimately? Honey, I love you. Thanks for supporting me, and allowing me to "run" every day.

For everyone else whose paths have crossed with mine, I thank you for teaching me the sales game -The world's oldest - and best - occupation!

Re-Introduction

What in the world was going on, a decade ago? In 2005, we published this book, for the first time, and struck a nerve with readers all over the world. I made a case for the theory that Sales IS the world's oldest profession (get your mind out of the gutter--prostitution is nothing but a Sales call), and.....wait for it.....everybody is in Sales! If you buy into my premise, whether you like it or not, and whether you sell a product, service, opinion, cause or even your teacher on an A instead of a B, you might as well learn to be good at it.

Some things remain the same in 2015--as we update and literally rewrite the book--though most things have changed. Before we build a whole new (Sales) structure, on our solid foundation of the Relationship Selling Process, I'd like to share a bit of history that has probably helped us chang our worldview of Sales and selling success. Be ready for a "game" of *That Was Then. This Is Now.* I'll be your Host for this edition of the show.

2005:

Michael Jackson is in the news as the King of Pop pleads not guilty to committing a lewd act upon a child.

Governor Arnold Schwarzenegger announces the imminent return of the *California Dream*.

The best place to live? According to The Economist, and their *quality of life* index for 111 countries, Ireland tops the list. (Q: Where's the best country to invest your money? A: Ireland, because the capital is always Dublin (doublin'--get it? A little author humor here)

Kodak was getting a little nervous, as "the age of *phon*ography" is under way, with cameras being overtaken and replaced by camera phones.

The bestselling business book for the year: *Good To Great* by Jim Collins--the same as the year before.

Two big risks threaten the economies around the world: a 40% surge in oil prices to $61 a barrel (what goes around....), and higher than expected interest rates (T-bills: 3.946%).

Hurricane Katrina showed that the World's leading super power was unprepared to deal with the aftermath of the natural disaster.

The trial of former Iraqi leader Saddam Hussein is under way, with many leaders wonder whether this would bring stability to the region or trigger a new wave of violence.

FINALLY: YouTube is launched in the United States. Need I say more?

In ten years, the world of Sales has changed dramatically and transformed completely, and that's why I've chosen this time to "overhaul" my first book: ***Life's A Sales Call: How To Succeed In The World's Oldest Profession***. At the end of the day, I hope you enjoy a decade's worth of tips, techniques and transformative behaviors that can up your game.

CONTENTS

Preface

How To Succeed in the World's Oldest Profession!

That's right! **Sales** -a job to many, career to others and avocation to a few of us, is the oldest profession in recorded history. Think about it. In fact, I challenge you to suggest an older one. For those of you thinking prostitution, that's just another type of sales call. Name the first sales person in recorded history (hint: female). If you answered, Eve, you' re right on. What was she selling? Fruit! Did she make the sale? Unfortunately, yes.

Few sales calls altered history as much as the first one in the Garden of Eden. Remember Moses' presentation upon descending Mt. Sinai with the Ten Commandments?

The world has always been moved by a compelling sales call.

Life's A Sales Call! If you're a professional, it doesn't matter what the title says on your business card, you're in sales. As such, you are the most important contributor in the world of business.

Why? Nothing happens until someone sells something.

If it weren't for those of us who sell for a living, the rest of the world would have nothing to do. There'd be no accountants, because there would be nothing to count; no laborers, since there'd be nothing to make; no service department - nothing to support; no maintenance workers -that's right- nothing to maintain!

2

Even if yours is not a conventional "selling" job, chances are strong you're still in sales. By the way, in any conversation, a sale is always made: Mom sells Junior on getting out of bed, or Junior sells Mom on sleeping in. Maybe you're a student. You're borderline A-B -after the final exam. You make an appointment to meet your professor after class. You know how hard you've worked -maybe he doesn't. Is there a name for this process? This is a sales call.

It matters not what you do or what you' re selling. It could be a product, service, concept, idea, grade, opinion or affiliation.

One reason I'd consider reading this book is if I had an interest in improving my "sales" percentage. In fact, this message goes out to two groups of people: those who sell for a living and those who don't. I dedicate this book to you, as you finally realize that you' re in sales -and you're never off the clock. Though I don't consider myself an expert per se, I'm a lifelong student of the (selling) craft. Malcolm Gladwell, mentions in his book, *Outliers: The Story of Success*, one definition of an expert: a person who invests a minimum of 10,000 hours, in a given subject--or for you Math majors--approximately 416 full days.

Best of luck to you, as you learn how to increase your odds in the sales game. ***Life's A Sales Call!*** Here's to your success in the pursuit!

Jack's Snack:

"A sales professional's job begins with a sale, it doesn't end with one".

Chapter 1

Robot or Relationship?

When was the last time that you were schmoozed? You know, when that charming, convincing man or woman led you ever so sweetly down the path of purchase. Or, maybe you were the schmoozer, walking away with another deal in your pocket. The thing about schmoozing is this: You can only schmooze for so long. It's an effective short ride - the art of psychological selling. Robot sales is like reciting the same poem over and over again. Relationship sales is reading a library of classical poetry. Robot sales is finite, relationship sales promises unlimited possibilities.

Relationship sales releases you to focus on the people you meet and the people you love. The beauty of it is, that as you build relationships, you build sales! If I were a schmoozer, the next thing I would say to you is, *Relationship sales is also easier than robot sales. You can master it in no time!* Well, that would be a lie. The fact is that relationship sales is far more difficult. The practice of developing relationships relies on you sharing your personal integrity. You actually have to maintain a quality relationship with yourself and with other people. It's one of the biggest challenges you will ever face. I know it has been a large challenge in life.

An entire industry is built on the art of the schmooze (sounds so superficial and manipulative, doesn't it?): tapes, phrases to memorize, tips on dress, body language and graduated pressure.

The problem with robot sales is that you'll make some money, but you won't watch it grow past a certain point, cuz robots don't grow--they stay the same size. The second problem with robot sales is what it does to you. How many robot salespeople have you known who live a life of constant pressure? Each month, they work to reach their goals: *More money. More money* is their silent mantra. Their smile frequently flattens out into a line of tension when a customer is not around. Here's a better mantra--compliments of Tony Robbins, Master Motivator: *I am enough. I do enough. I have enough.* I find myself repeating it, almost daily, though I still choke on the "have enough" thang.

Ask yourself this: What other process will reap such rewards: personal happiness, ever-increasing wealth and ever-increasing satisfaction in your interactions with people? I'd do it all again, even if it was three times more effort. The wealth I've earned internally and externally has been worth every ounce of energy and attention I've committed to developing relationship sales process.

So, I want to put this question to you, not as a schmoozer, but as a fellow human being -are you ready to begin the process of becoming a successful relationship-centered/centric person?

ONE DECADE LATER

The greatest challenge of Relationship-centric professionals: converting *research* to *relationships*, and relationships to *revenue streams*. Research? In today's "internet world", there are no secrets. Of course, that's a good news/bad news scenario, depending on your purpose. The good news: you can learn almost anything about anyone, anytime. Just reach for the "Cloud". You know your buyers are researching you, and your company. In fact, CEB (Corporate Executive Board) studies prove, that today, before you are contacted, 57%--or more--of the purchase decision has already been made. Conversely, don't even think about making contact with Mr(s) Decision-Maker, without doing some preliminary research. Try my "3 for 3" suggestion: before meeting anyone, invest three minutes, minimum, to learn three unique things about them. A great place to start is always Linkedin. Follow that up with a Google search for the person, and his/her firm. The bad news: *you* have no secrets, either. You wanna be amused? Google yourself when you have time. You may even learn something.

Nothing compresses the relationship process faster, than finding those areas you have in common, with your current candidates or future customers. You build from here. Relationship building is always a marathon and never a sprint, and regardless of how long it takes you, your relationship-building challenge is just beginning! Many are Masters (at this stage), yet the greatest hill to climb occurs next: converting your new friend to a customer--or revenue stream. Jeffrey Gitomer, a contemporary and acquaintance of mine, wrote one of my favorite sales books: *The Sales Bible*. Add it to your

8

personal library. In it, Jeffrey claims that more than half of your customers will be considered friends. So his theory is that *we don't need more prospects (candidates), we need more friends.* Become a Master at moving your friends towards customer status. Oh, and that starts with asking for the order. You'll learn, later on in this book, one of my all-time favorite Jack's Snacks: *If you don't A.S.K., you don't G.E.T.* Or if you really depend on making sales for a living, *If you don't A.S.K., you don't E.A.T.* Ask!

Jack's Snack:

"Doubt whom you will, but never yourself".

Chapter 2

You Are The Source

You said, YES and that's why you're reading Chapter Two. Good for you! Most things worth having are worth asking for, and I'm glad you've decided to work towards adding sales to your pursuit of a balanced life. That's right, relationship sales is about more than making money, it's about making money while having deep, satisfying relationships, throughout your life. It's about making more money and increasing the trust, intimacy, balance and successful conflict resolution throughout your life. That's why the title of this book is **Life's a Sales Call**. It's a book that acknowledges the importance of living a balanced life, which includes *affluence*--measured in your terms.

I have a single woman friend who makes a quick study of each man that she meets for a date by finding out how he treats himself. For instance, she says that if he's frazzled and overworked, she knows that he would probably ignore her needs, since he is ignoring his own. If he's overweight or smokes, she knows that the time may come when he treats her with disrespect since he is treating his body with disrespect. The key to successful relationships starts with the relationship you have with yourself. The key to successful sales is the depth of your relationships. It's clear where the source of your prosperity lies. You are the source.

Your relationship with yourself is the template of all your other relationships - personal or professional. As you progress in this book through the twelve different aspects of a good

12

relationship, the first place you will focus is on your relationship with yourself. I have shared my own inner struggles with you to provide an example and also because in writing this book, I am entering into a relationship with you. My openness with you is my way of saying that I trust you. I hope that you will return my trust and invest in yourself. Over time, your investment will yield tremendous results.

Once you are right with you, you can turn your attention to other people, with confidence. Each step that you consciously take toward respect, accountability and trust is a step towards the wealth of a lifetime. The time and attention that you sincerely give to other people will boomerang back to you, exponentially. This book is designed to help guide you in connecting with yourself, and connecting with others. Life is a sales call. Each person that you meet, however trivial you may feel the interaction to be, is important. They may be a family member, a friend, a client or a stranger. Take a deep breath. Look into their eyes, smile and listen. Let time pass without anxiety. It is only through the passage of time that true connections are made. If you do not have the time to invest in others, you will not have relationships of substance, over the long haul.

From this point forward, each chapter in the book starts with a letter from the word R.E.L.A.T.I.O.N.S.H.I.P.--in sequence. I wanted to make this message as clear and straightforward for you as possible. The first section of each chapter will define the concept, such as respect, following this page. In the second section, I share personal struggles, either mine or others, in the pursuit of developing a relationship. The third section in each chapter will focus on relationships with others, and includes an example from either my life or the life of someone close to me. The fourth section provides you with a next step--an action that you can take, to move you closer to your goal of becoming a relationship-centered person. Finally, I leave you with some basic building blocks to a successful life--based on YOUR definition, not mine.

If you're ready, I'm ready. Let's begin!

Jack's Snack:

"You never get a second chance at a first impression".

Chapter 3

Respectful

Respect, in my mind, includes a degree of kindness. Sometimes, respect also includes admiration. I've heard many couples-- blissfully married--say that respect, more than anything else, is responsible for keeping their marriages intact. I'm reminded of Aretha Franklin's first track on the album, *I Never Loved A Man The Way I Love You*, written by Otis Redding: *R.E.S.P.E.C.T.* You may recall the lyrics, *R-E-S-P-E-C-T. Find out what it means to me. R-E-S-P-E-C-T. Take care TCB* (taking care of business). She's just asking for a little respect in her life, as it means so much to her. What does it mean to you?

The knowledge that someone else thinks well of you is the foundation for any lasting relationship, including a customer relationship. Before you can speak or act respectfully toward another human being, you must look upon yourself, with compassion and kindness. Each day, you must face yourself and say, *I'm a good person. I'm a remarkable person. I believe in me completely.* When denigrating voices begin to surface in your consciousness, it is imperative to answer them with a strong, clear statement that reflects the deep regard you hold for yourself.

Going Within:

Jack's Inside Guy

Do you ever hear a voice in your head? A voice saying something like this, *You're a loser. What's wrong with you--you poseur?* How do you respond? For a long time, I silently answered, *Yes, I must be a poser. Something is wrong with me. I'm not being honest with myself.* In this silent, internal dialogue, I consistently treated myself with disrespect. I'll never forget Labor Day weekend, September 1-4, 2000. It marked the beginning of a long, ongoing conversation, playing in my head. As a result, I entered a sustained sales slump.

That weekend, I bought out the final partner in *Diamond Warkenthien Swindall*, our Sales Advisory Company, founded in 1995--Clint Swindall, and renamed my new wholly-owned business *NextStep Solutions*. Now, the business was now all mine, effective September 1, 2000. Wow! I became a solo business owner/entrepreneur, for the first time in my professional life.

Along with the earnings possibilities, I soon realized that I also owned the remaining outstanding business debt - exceeding $50,000 at the time. In valuing the transaction, I had overlooked this debt when calculating how much money the assets were worth. Oops. At the end of the day, after all of the papers were signed, I recognized my "valuation" mistake.

I felt like such a chump! Pride kept me from broaching the subject with my former business partner, for fear I'd expose myself as an ignorant owner. I was embarrassed and mad at myself. My solution was to just beat myself up - emotionally - over the next two years, as I tried to dig out of the hole I created. Each day, instead of accepting the fact that I am a decent person who made a mistake, like many emerging entrepreneurs are prone to do, I said to myself, *Jack, you're a loser. What's wrong with you, Mr. Big Pockets?*

By allowing this subconscious conversation to continue, I lost a little respect for myself, and saw my swagger leave town on the next rail out.

Without being respectful -of myself -I had a hard time selling anything, especially me. I felt like a poseur. For the first time, I didn't like the product I was selling. In fact, I lost confidence in who I was and what I did as a sales specialist, and worse, I was having trouble getting over it.

Then, something happened, and I can't take any credit for the timing. A local, prominent business leader came to me looking for sales help. He was referred by a mutual friend of ours. My first thought was, *Great. I'm glad he sees something in me. I sure don't!* In less than a month, due to a one-year consulting and sales training project, NextStep Solutions was cash - flowing again. My confidence soared, as positive results occurred for our newest--and largest--client.

His respect for me, reminded me that I am more than a compilation of my mistakes. From that point forward, when that voice in my head begins to say, *You're a loser. What's wrong with you?* I counter the argument by thinking, *I am a worthy, successful human being and business professional, and none of my mistakes can ever change that.*

Fast forward to January, 2010, just over five years, since I experienced most of life's significant emotional events (S.E.E.), starting December 13, 2004, when I started my run as a radio personality on the *BizRadio Network: The Sound of Your Money Growing*, and V.P. of Sales, for this fledgling radio startup headquartered in Houston. The opportunity required a physical move to Houston, from my home of sixteen years in San Antonio. Rather than moving the family immediately, I decided to test the waters first, so I rented an apartment, literally across the street from the radio station. After all, I justified, Houston is just three driving hours away from S.A. and I'd be returning on most weekends. Huge mistake, by the way, as I demonstrated a lack of commitment to the new opportunity.

OK. Allow me to review the "scorecard": *New career* (I kept NextStep Solutions functioning, while I diverted my personal efforts--can you say hedging my bet?)--that was S.E.E. number one. New town (I was involved, yet not committed)--S.E.E. number two. 3. New marital status (separated from my wife)-- S.E.E. number three. In retrospect, this sequence was THE most selfish, self-centered series of decisions, I had ever made in my life.

Here I was, grabbing at the proverbial brass ring once again, subordinating or ignoring everyone else I loved in my life. It was all me. I've never been uncomfortable in being alone, but this was different. I was lonely as it was me against a (new) world. I forgot that life, as in sales, is a team sport, and I blew off my team. Those voices returned, shaking my being to the core, and knocking all my confidence, down and out. *Now, what have I got myself into?* Ironically, I kept thinking of a bright side, as in, *this is gonna be great fodder for my next book.*

19

Well, the journey with BizRadio concluded in five years, and I was back to where I was, before this selfish experiment began-- none the richer--and now I was scrambling furiously to replace the cash flow I had enjoyed, during my stint. There's nothing more deflating in life, than facing the prospects of starting over, now as a fifty-something professional.

Reaching Out:

Planting Seeds in the Dark

A very dear friend, I'll call "Andy" suffered a hard financial hit earlier in the year. Andy had to absorb a nearly $45,000 loss, as a result of someone else's mistake, at his firm. As a financial planner and investment sage, even when a securities trading error occurs, Andy is responsible for the fallout and is fully accountable to his client.

Andy's assistant did not follow through on the requested trades of a client. When a significant change occurred in the value of the stock - the shortfall had to be made up in the investment portfolio. What is worse, the client needed to be made aware of the scenario for SEC reasons. At the end of the day, Andy chose the high road and never showed any disrespect towards his assistant, who was devastated, emotionally--far more so than Andy.

Andy's deep sense of ethics and moral accountability kept him at peace. Andy expects the highest standards of behavior from himself. When his operation suffered a glitch, he took responsibility for it. Andy respects his assistant. He knows that she is worth supporting and that she is not defined by her mistakes. Finally, as a result of his own self-respect, Andy respected his client enough to tell him the truth, and enough to show vulnerability to another person.

In real life, the more likely scenario often plays out: fire the assistant, garnish her last paycheck, and try to rationalize the crisis away, to the client, blaming her for all the problems. I asked Andy if he ever considered this alternative. *"Never", he countered, "not even for a moment!"*

I have already seen Andy enjoy a sequence of positive results, due to his actions in this situation. We reap what we sow, though we often cannot see, when we plant the "seed of respect" in darkness, nor do we ever know how it will bloom in the light of day.

The Next Step

Write a letter to yourself and mail it from the post office to your home. In the letter, articulate your gratitude, admiration and *respect* for yourself. List your accomplishments, and the items you wish to accomplish. Mention your strengths and the skills that you have, to make your goals a reality. Now, upon receipt, sit down with a friend or loved one and share the contents of the letter.

Once you have received and read that letter, sit down to write another one. This time, write a letter to a friend, family member or business associate that you know well. Express in the letter the same kind of gratitude, admiration and respect, for *them*. List the things that you've seen them accomplish and how they have had a positive impact on you. You can choose to mail the letter or not mail it, depending upon how vulnerable you want to be. Let me point out, however, that the more vulnerable you are willing to be in your relationships with others, the more successful your relationships will be.

Building Blocks to Successful Sales

We have been doing it all wrong! Most of us have been taught how to sell, in a way that directly contrasts to how customers really buy. Even IBM--my first corporate job--taught us, *The Logical Selling Process*. It may have been logical to the highly-paid IBM faculty, and like most other Sales training platforms, it resembled a snowman (visualize four balls that comprise a snowman with the head being the smallest (Discovering-10%), the next ball being slightly larger (Matching-20%), followed by even a slightly bigger circle (Resolving-30%) and the base being the largest (CLOSING-40%). The four words in parenthesis are the words that define the four steps we use, during any sales situation--and the approximate amount of time we invest in that segment. In reality, we should turn the snowman upside down and reverse the percentage of time, invested in each stage of the sales process. Said another way, we should invest 40% of our time *Discovering* (the needs of our customers) and 10% of our time *OPENING* (aka Closing) the account, relationship, case, or whatever you call it. The selling process must mirror the buying process. Like any good relationship, you must both give and receive and sales by definition, is a relationship not a transaction.

Ask them questions about their area of expertise and *discover* who they are as a person. In exchange, show a real interest in how you can be of service to them.

Once you have *opened* a sale with a customer, then you have begun your relationship with them. From that moment on, you are involved in maintaining a relationship with that person.

24

They may buy from you again or they may not. Be assured, however, that if you employ each of the characteristics and actions in this book as you interact with them, they will enrich both your life and your business.

The first building block to building the kinds of relationships that lead to sales success, is a balanced approach to sales excellence, or BASE. The word, balance is tossed around a lot these days but what does it really mean? I think that it refers to each ingredient of a person's life, and understood on a routine basis. These five areas are: Spiritual, Physical, Psychological, Personal and Professional. So, on a routine basis, you will need to exercise, develop your mind through reading and inquiry, connect with the Spiritual or divine presence and express your emotions in a clear and healthy way. If you have an addiction in your life such as smoking, drinking, gambling etc. now is the time to seriously consider eradicating that addiction from your life. As long as you are addicted, you are not balanced because addictions cover up emotions and they compromise our health.

Entire books have been written about balance. I will take a moment here to say that the primary building blocks that build everything I talk about here, are your values. What are your values? One of my main values is family and another one is financial security. I have a friend who values creativity and good health as primary priorities. You can look at other people's lives and easily see what their values are. A man and woman who work over sixty hours a week, and have two neglected children, probably value financial security or professional achievement, over family. A person who jogs everyday and eats junk food for most meals values quick gratification over health, even though they exercise. It's easy to see what other people's values are.

Try to take an objective look at yourself and write down at least three core values.

The second building block is a clear vision. I can't stress how important this is! Your vision is your way of truly creating what you want. Sit down every day for a week and write out a description of your vivid vision.

Describe the vision of your days, your business dealings, what you are doing with your money, your relationships and accomplishments, that lead to achieving your vision. I see not only goals but also how I will live each day, in terms of my living arrangements, social engagements, financial transactions, travel, conversations etc. For instance, let's say that you have a vision of traveling for your business. You're also a single parent. Create a vision that provides a way for your child to have a fantastic caregiver while you are working. Describe the qualities this person will have. Do the same thing for everything that matters to you in your life. The clearer your vision, the better! Why? When you create a clear vision of what you want, your vision will push itself into reality.

The third building block is a concrete plan. As you visualize, take one step at a time--ones that will eventually lead to your goals being accomplished. A concrete plan lends structure and viability to your vision. It is a vital component in creating balance because it relies on structure. While honoring your imagination, from which all good business ideas come, with a clear vision, you must also build the mechanism, a plan, to actualize the vision.

Goals, of course, are baked into your plan. No matter what you want to achieve, you can do it through establishing goals. Goals are nothing more than a way for us to practice self-discipline daily. When we put deadlines on our dreams, we put wings on our dreams.

Here is an example of a S.M.A.R.T. goal:

A professional goal for me would be to focus on penetrating the wholesale packaging industry as a sales advisor/trainer/consultant. That for me, is a niche and a *specific* goal (the **S** in S.M.A.R.T.) Your goal must be very specific. Another more specific goal I had, when I hosted a LIVE radio show: I wanted to syndicate the show, *Your Next Step Towards Success*, starting in Houston and Dallas, where I was already on the air, and move out in both directions across the country.

To make my goal measurable (the **M** in S.M.A.R.T.), I want the dollar value of my business relationships to begin at $100,000.00 (recurring revenue streams) and move towards two million dollars, over the course of thirty months. I intended to open three new client accounts by the end of one year and support ten clients by the end of two and a half years. I write down these goals and the dates by which I will achieve them.

Then, I take action, in my mind, moving towards my goal, with a declarative statement, like the following: *I WILL focus on the industrial packaging industry, and open three new accounts, on or before.......*(insert date). Hence, the **A** (in S.M.A.R.T.) stands for action-oriented, in the first-person.

The **R** in S.M.A.R.T stands for *realistic*. Sometimes, we get carried away with our goals. If you wrote that you will increase your client base by five hundred times within a two week period, you may need a reality check. Make sure that your goals are actually reachable in YOUR estimation, or they will become disincentives for you.

Finally, **T** stands for *timely*. "Someday" is not timely. Neither is "around ten years from now." Let your goal have a clear start and stop date, preferably completed within a one to three year period of time.

Each goal requires quantifiable or measurable results, and dates by which those results will be achieved and action statements that lead you to achieving the results. You're going to be doing a bit of writing for just one year. Keep your calendar and calculator handy. You will find that these pieces of paper become your touchstones as you move methodically toward your success.

Oh, I almost forgot! One of the most important aspects of creating your goals is to share them with others. Ask for support and buy-in from your colleagues, friends and families. Carry your goals with you always. Each day, read your goals out loud to yourself. Just hearing them will move you toward them faster.

Jack's Snack:

"The depth of your convictions is more important than the length of your knowledge".

Chapter 4

Enthusiastic

Enthusiasm is a deal-maker or a deal breaker. You may have all the financial backing, letters of recommendation and beautiful marketing materials in the world, but if you lack enthusiasm, your resources may be money down the drain. That doesn't just go for the business world, that applies to all undertakings, relative to relationships. Remember how excited you felt in the beginning of your current job, marriage or when your child was born? That enthusiasm is truly the wind beneath your wings. The ability to picture the positive possibilities and feel happy and energized by your word picture is a spark of gold that brings light, hope and joy to any undertaking.

ONE DECADE LATER

Today, more than ever, all buying decisions are based on emotion, and justified with logic. You'll read this throughout the book, and I can't emphasize the point too much. Having started my professional sales career with a computer company, then later moving to a software company, post-IBM, and finally joining a digital marketing communications firm, I experienced numerous business cultures that emphasized technology, intellectual property, and the strategy of selling to technocrats or engineers. The feat is possible, but often more difficult and time-consuming. Sales isn't rocket science, it's *neuroscience* (we'll expand on that thought later on). The word Enthusiasm comes from the Greek word enthousiasmos, or "en-theos", meaning "the god within". Do you share your enthusiasm?

Nothing inspires purchasing decisions more, than you sharing your deep convictions for your company, service or product. In fact, the word Inspire has Latin roots, inspirare, "in" plus "spirare" (breathe), related to spiritus, "breath of life". If you sell the heart, the mind will follow--it's not the other way around. Today, science will support this premise.

Going Within:

Cancelled? I Don't Think So!

What's the point of being enthusiastic? Doesn't it make you a bit of a pain in a world of deadpan pragmatists? The point is that enthusiasm is a wave. It's a wave that carries you from disappointment to triumph. My story about enthusiasm has to do with two things that I am passionate about: radio (or the theater of the mind as I like to call it) and expanding one's influence.

July 12, 2003 -a day of answered prayer. There must be something to the now famous *Prayer of Jabez*, an obscure book in the Bible: *Oh that you would bless me, indeed and enlarge my territory, that your hand would be with me, and that you would keep me from evil, that I may not cause pain* (1 Chronicles 4:10). It is a memorable verse--though obscure--that often takes its place at the beginning of my daily recital. The difference that day: my radio show, *Life's A Sales Call!* was introduced on *KSLR AM/630: The WORD in South Texas*. Talk about expanding my territory! I began broadcasting to thirty-seven counties in South Texas and a population base of up to four million listeners. FOUR MILLION! Not that the entire population of South Texas listened to me every Saturday...but they could!

As a latecomer to the one-hour business talk radio show arena, my goal was to *inform, educate, recognize and entertain* all who cared to tune in. I dreamed of being the "Rush Limbaugh of Business Radio", with a nationally syndicated show, reaching out to like souls -small and home business professionals, mostly. Starting in July of 2003, every Saturday morning at eleven in the morning, I trekked into the San Antonio studio and delivered my message. I often invited a guest to join me on the air, who I'd interview as the subject matter expert that day.

I am fond of saying, *The depth of one's convictions is more important than the length of one's knowledge.* What that meant, as it applied to me, is that I did not even pretend to know all the answers. Nevertheless, I enthusiastically asked questions that penetrated to the heart of each topic.

As the year progressed, I gained confidence--and listeners -and just knew that it was now only a matter of time before I was discovered! People called in, emailed, even wrote letters, asking for transcripts of our shows (www.lifesasalescall.com). As we approached our first anniversary on the air with over forty shows in the *can*, it was time to talk contract renewal.

That's when I received "The Letter." It was from the new General Manager of the station, thanking me for a great year on the air and informing me that the show, *Life's A Sales Call!* was not going to be renewed.

Apparently, the Salem Radio Network brain trust, were not as enthusiastic as I was, about my future on radio. That's O.K. because my enthusiasm carried me through that disappointment and on to a new opportunity. Can you say, *The BizRadio Network--The Sound of your Money Growing?*

Reaching Out:

Changing Lives With Positive Energy

I've never met a baby-sitter like him -ever. For several years, I was blessed to engage Steve Crellin as my three boys -two years apart -were growing up. Steve was one motivated teenager, who enthusiastically threw himself into every situation, whether it was high school or promoting his baby-sitter services in the neighborhood we all lived. Toward the end of our two-year "window", Steve was getting pretty popular with the neighbors, so we had to reserve him early.

If you asked any of the boys at the time, *Who do you want, to babysit?* there'd be an immediate response in one breath: *Steve!*. You see, Steve was all about making a difference, not making money. You could say that he was just plain enthusiastic about life, and passionate about his "clients".

He led by example, always being *more* polite then his peers. What made him stand out? Steve was a true marketer. His between - gig visits to the house, to see if Nick, Ross or Will wanted to play. He'd bring gifts over, on their birthdays. Steve *wanted* to be around our boys, and his enthusiasm for nurturing their relationship was contagious. Steve went on, to finish a stint in the U.S. Coast Guard, married and moved to California. For years thereafter, we'd get cards and letters from him, and we stayed in touch with his family, the Crellins who resided in our neighborhood, at the time.

When the kids needed a role model, friend or confidant they would go see Steve. He touched my sons in ways that few

34

others ever knew. For a couple of years, Steve was the "gold standard" by which all others were measured. We knew, with certainty, that our sons were better prepared for life, after being draped in the enthusiastic "blanket" of their favorite babysitter -Steve!

The Next Step

Enthusiasm in sales translates into genuine, sincere interest in your client. Stop the habit of talking about yourself. Be genuinely interested in learning about your client and in acknowledging them in creative, thoughtful ways. One practice that I have is to quickly gauge the energy level of my client and gear my own energy level up or down to match theirs. Here's a story of an expert salesman who received a lesson in the value of enthusiastic interest from his secretary.

This individual had won numerous awards in his company and in his city as the top salesperson of the year for two years in a row. He is a low-keyed person who pays attention to what he's hearing and saying at all times. He has one passionate hobby and that is revamping vintage sports cars. A television show about extreme makeovers of cars called, *Pimp My Ride* is his all-time favorite show.

One day, this man was sitting in his office when his secretary entered the room carrying a big box with a beautiful bow on top. He opened the card and read, *We think the world of you*.

Inside of the box were three DVDs of the *Pimp My Ride* show as well as a *Pimp My Ride* T-shirt.

This veteran salesman was deeply impressed with the level of effort that his secretary had gone to, in order to give him such a meaningful and personal gift.

Channel your enthusiasm into getting to know each of your clients so well that you know what their passions are in life.

Then, make it a point to personalize your conversations and gifts to them to show how enthusiastic you are about working with them.

Building Blocks to Successful Sales

I don't know about you, but the way that I can detect someone's interest in me and enthusiasm for knowing me, is by observing how curious they are about me. Conversely, a potential client is going to pick up your interest in *them* if you are genuinely curious. As you scan today's bestseller list, you'll find one of my recent favorite reads, *A Curious Mind: The Secret To A Bigger Life*, by Brian Grazer. You may know him as the producer of *A Beautiful Mind, Apollo 13, Splash, 8 Mile*, and tons of others. He usually works in tandem with Ron Howard, (aka Opie), who directs most of his films. Brian's premise: we are living in the golden age of curiosity and his enthusiasm to talk to anyone and everyone, opens a world of creativity and adventure. I loved the book.

Being curious is a great way to get to know someone and in the process qualify him or her as a viable customer or not. While you want to be relaxed and human in your interactions with others, the more questions that you ask, specifically relating to them and their long-term needs, the more time you can save in the selling process.

I told you about my Lady friend, who can tell how a man might treat her, by how he treats himself. Well, this same friend makes a point of asking specific questions when she first meets a man, (i.e. "What sort of relationship do you have with your family?"). From his answers she can decide if she wants to spend any more time with him.

Sales is very much like dating. Why spend an hour having dinner when you can discern in five to twenty minutes, that it's probably not a match?

You want to find out four things from your potential customer:

1. *What are their primary needs?*
2. *What is their decision-making process?*
3. *From who else are they considering purchasing?*
4. *What concerns do they have that you haven't discussed?*

The time that you invest learning about a potential customer's wants and needs sends them a signal that the buying process is a collaborative one. You are *discovering* exactly what they need and perhaps you can provide that product or service to them. Regardless, they will know that your goal is to help them get the best solution, not to simply sell your product, and separate them from their money.

I had a potential client call me the other day. After we talked for a few minutes, I realized that my client needed someone with a very specific kind of real estate background. I was quickly able to refer her to a friend of mine and didn't waste any time at all. I demonstrated our N.E.E.R. Marketing Strategy (Networking of Existing Economic Relationships), while supporting a colleague, created a referral opportunity while learning a little bit more about a niche market of which I was totally unaware.

These days, I like to think that I can talk to someone for about five minutes and tell you whether they are an *amiable, expressive, analytical or driver* personality. Each personality type has a different level of emotional expression, assertiveness and interest in human interaction. Trying to trade jokes before getting down to business with a driver may irritate your potential client. On the other hand, starting a meeting without a personal conversation of some kind will irritate and confuse an expressive personality. Take the time to sort out different ways to subtly interact with varied personality types.

The person with an amiable personality tends to show a low degree of assertiveness and a high degree of emotional expression. Amiable personalities are responsive and friendly. An amiable is most concerned about stability. Knowing that your potential client has an amiable personality will allow you to address stability first with them. It will also allow you to gear your own emotional expression up and your level of assertiveness down.

Remember, an amiable may want security, sincere appreciation, repeated work patterns, time to adjust to change, limited territory of responsibility, identification with the group and areas of specialization.

Those people who have an expressive personality tend to have a high degree of assertiveness and a high degree of emotional expression. Expressive personalities are outgoing and persuasive, and prefer to work with other people. The like the spotlight and enjoy doing what they are good at. An expressive personality is most concerned about acceptance.

Remember, an expressive may want social system and acceptance, freedom from details, people to talk to, positive working conditions, recognition for abilities and the opportunity to inspire and influence others.

Those people who have an analytical personality tend to have a low degree of assertiveness and a low degree of emotional expression. Analytical personalities focus on facts more than feelings. They evaluate situations objectively and gather lots of data before making a decision. They prefer organization and specific expectations. An analytical personality is most concerned about accuracy.

Remember, an analytical personality may want autonomy and independence, controlled work environments, reassurance, precise expectations and goals, exact job descriptions and planned change.

Those people who have a driver personality tend to have a high degree of assertiveness and a low degree of emotional expression. They know what they want and how they intend to get it. They manage tasks well and are very results oriented. They thrive on competition and don't like to lose. A driver is most concerned about time.

Remember that a driver may want authority, varied activities, prestige, freedom from assignments, promoting growth, "bottom line" approach and opportunity for advancement.

Take notes and learn how to identify each personality. Customize the way that you interact with each personality type based on what you know they respond to the most. For instance, when you are talking with a person who has an amiable personality avoid being confrontational. Instead, clearly define goals and assure them of your follow-up support.

When you are talking with a person who has an expressive personality avoid telling them what to do and be sure to allow them to express all of their ideas to you. Make a point of developing a participative relationship.

When you are talking with a person who has an analytical personality always answer questions with through detail. Try to be as specific as possible in your speech and support what you say with accurate data.

When you are talking with a driver personality, stay away from generalizations or very sociable behavior. Instead, focus on business and results. Be positive and highlight the logical benefits of the ideas and approaches you are presenting.

Some people may qualify as clients but they're just not interested. This is not so bad, because it gives you the opportunity to be curious. "What are a few reasons why you would not choose to open a relationship with me today?"

Some people may be interested but they just don't qualify and some will be both interested and qualified. Only a fraction of those people whom you have qualified will actually open a relationship with you. That is why it is so important to save time and energy when you sell by asking clear, specific questions as soon as possible. Here are a few that I find helpful to me:

"What sort of budget are you working with?"

"Who makes the decisions in your organization?"

"What alternatives are you considering?"

You get the idea! Here's one of my favorites, "What is the likelihood of you establishing a long-term, mutually beneficial, prosperous relationship with me?"

Open-ended questions ask your potential client to just talk about their business or their past experiences. This allows you to get an idea of what sort of opportunities their organization has to offer.

Closed-ended questions have clear Yes and No answers such as, "Yes, we have an internal training staff," or "No, we don't own our warehouses."

Tactical questions have more to do with the client's interaction with you and come after you have opened a relationship. You are asking them if they are still planning on X, if the service they chose worked well for them or what their thoughts are on upgrading now that they've used the first level of service. These questions help you confirm what you already know or gather new information. Tactical questions show your commitment to this client and to their satisfaction. They discover how the customer feels about the product or service they purchased and if they would consider making another commitment in the future.

If time is really short, just cut to the chase and find out if *cost, quality or service* is the most important thing to them. Whatever they answer gives you a quick picture of the potential of this sale and what their dominant buying motive is. I suggest that you decide ahead of time how you want to respond to each of these priorities.

It takes time, attention and real enthusiasm to learn how and when to ask questions of clients and potential clients. Doing your homework allows you to quickly qualify individuals and move to the next step with them.

Time is all that you have, so use it wisely to research, ask, listen and respond in a way that builds relationship and builds business easily and naturally. *Life's A Sales Call!* This is your life that you're investing. Invest it with gusto and engage with other human beings in a genuine way and you will be doing nothing less than having fun and making money at the same time!

Jack's Snack"

"It is better to be interested than to be interesting".

Chapter 5

Likeable

To have a friend, you have to be a friend. I'm not sure of the origin of that last sentence, but it makes sense to me. Think of BLT sandwiches: *believable, likeable and trustworthy.* We're in the business of selling sandwiches--BLTs! Likeability is a kind of intuitive mirroring. You meet someone and you figure out what parts of you fit with who they are. You pull those parts out and make them shine, then you create affinity. Not everybody has learned how to listen at this level and respond naturally. I encourage you to practice being likeable with people you meet, especially those people who do not appear at first to have much in common with you. Step one is to simply be curious. Ask questions and find out more about the person in front of you that you perceive as being different from you.

What I'm suggesting to you is that you expand your comfort zone considerably, one conversation at time. Expanding one's comfort zone is by definition, uncomfortable. I suggest that you accept the reality of feeling discomfort as you begin to relate on a deeper level with everyone that you encounter. Eventually, you will find that you've gone from being a piece of kite string to being a rubber band. As people respond to what they see in you, you will even start to like yourself more as well. I challenge you to try on this new behavior and see what happens.

Going Within:

Celebrate Differences!

One of my dear friends, from my Fighting Illini and Delta Sigma Phi era, Les Huls, doesn't have much in common with me. He lives in another state and is a farm boy. I am a city dweller, born and bred. While I'm a rather intense person, Les is quiet and laid-back. I speak before rooms of people; Les works quietly in an office as a city planner. Our rhythms are very different and I think it is this difference that has made our friendship so lasting. Every time Les and I speak, I come away with a new and refreshing perspective. He provides me with a new perspective, because we both value the other person's differences, we share a strong bond of friendship that has lasted over forty years.

Reaching Out:

Likeability in Action

I graduated from the University of Illinois in Champaign-Urbana, Illinois. Back then, the fraternity houses had open-air dorms. This means that sleeping bunks were outside of our rooms in the hallways. Though we slept in a bunk room, we still each had a residence and usually a roommate. My freshman year roommate was Barry Robinson. Barry was a junior transfer student from a nearby town in Illinois called Gibson City. While Barry was a small town guy, I came from a big city. On the surface, we didn't have much in common. Over that year and the next, however, I came to think of Barry and me as big brother/little brother. He took me out to the Gibson City October fest and did what Barry did best, hang out, drink beer and talk to pretty ladies. While our conversations back then were pretty shallow, I nevertheless learned a valuable lesson from Barry about being likeable. Barry instinctively found the point of common interest in anyone he met, including me. While not everyone was his *best* friend, almost everyone who met Barry liked him.

The Next Step

Think about the individuals who are fixtures in your life. Make a point to remember those that may seem invisible to you like your next door neighbor, your receptionist or your broker. Now, mentally visualize the people you plan to meet in the coming week.

I want you to make a commitment to yourself that every single person that you meet, familiar or new, you will stop, focus and discover what you have in common. This means that you will need to move more slowly through your day and that you will need to develop the habit of asking questions. This exercise is going to be something of a strain for you but I want you to put your focus each and every time on someone else. Try not to walk away until you have found what you have in common with the other person. How many questions did it take until you discovered something? Was this easy for you? What experiences did you have? I'd like to know!

E-mail me at jack@lifesasalescall.com.

Building Blocks to Successful Sales

I have often heard potential clients say, "What's in it for me?" If they don't say it, most are still thinking it. In fact, most people's favorite radio station is WII/FM, or "What's in it for me?" They will jump over your desk to find the tuner on your radio! Let me translate that phrase: "Does the value of your solution exceed my investment in it?" We've just talked about being likeable and that means finding a point of common interest.

When it comes down to your business relationship with someone and providing him or her with avaluable solution, it's up to you to discover the "launch pad" of common benefit that you share with your customer.

This is where your research, training and disciplined questions have led you. They have led you to the point of fully understanding your customer's need enough to propose a solution for it that will prove so valuable to them that it will be worth the money they invest.

Now, after having the privilege of hosting a daily, live talk radio show for over five years, I discovered peoples' favorite AM station. And NO, it wasn't my show, "Where Wall Street Meets Main Street". Rather, it was MMFG/AM, or "make me feel good, about myself". You want to find ways to make the other party feel good about themselves, their life, profession, family, or anything else. Usually a tasteful compliment or sincere observation fills the bill. My goal was to get them to say to themselves: "I like myself best, when I'm with Jack, because he makes me feel good about myself. Heaven knows everyone needs positive strokes in their life, and few are ever given from others. Pass'em out. They're FREE and widely available in unlimited supply!

Pay attention to this matching process because it can make you or break you! Thoroughly understand the nature of the client's problem. Hasty judgments and proposals can lead to lost revenue, time and good will all the way around. Here are five steps that I follow:

1. Develop a deep understanding of your products and services.
2. Determine the advantages of what you have to offer (This usually includes understanding your competitors' weak points.)
3. Collect evidence of your past successes such as testimonials, case studies and reference names.
4. State in a clear, simple way how the value of what you have to offer fits perfectly with the need your client is demonstrating.
5. Gain the client's commitment to relying on you to provide a solution for their problems.

The F-A-B-R-E Filter

F-A-B-R-E is actually an acronym and a vital component of the Matching step in sales.

When I meet with candidates, the first thing I do is explain to them what the Features are of my service. I provide a variety of different types of training and consultations. I also provide one-on-one coaching geared toward sales, service, leadership and opening relationships.

When my future client fully understands what I have to offer, I point out the Advantages of using me over other providers. We are unique in our process and approach and I know exactly how in relation to other sales trainers and the various alternatives available.

I make the advantages very clear and move on to the Benefits that they will receive from opening a relationship with me. When I talk about benefits, I'm suggesting what's in it for them. I'm explaining how the value of what they will receive, exceeds the investment they make to receive that value. I ensure that my potential customer understands that they are getting great value.

The two most powerful motivators for any decision are *PAIN* and *PLEASURE,* in that order. In fact, in descending order, you must demonstrate how you will remove pain, prevent pain, provide pleasure or promise future pleasure. You must discover where their priority is, among these areas. They each provide a "motive-for-action" or what we commonly call motivation.

Right about then in the conversation, I sit back in my chair and give the customer the opportunity to share a response to what I have presented. I ask them, *Does this sound like something of interest to you?* When I do this, I am communicating this message: getting this sale is less important to me than providing you with the exact solution you need. I'm open to walking away from the offer, if you don't agree that we have a *match*. The ability to release the sale and live with the possibility of not receiving their business makes the interaction relaxed and authentic. Only when you are sincerely concerned for the client's best interest will they seriously consider what you have to offer.

Finally, I provide them with tangible Evidence that I can deliver what I say I can deliver. I give them names and phone numbers of happy customers, show them testimonial letters, as well as company progress reports showing increases in sales following my training. I encourage my clients to question me and investigate me freely. I want them to feel that we are a perfect match.

Being likeable really boils down to two things: paying attention and being flexible. If you have created an environment between yourself and your potential customer where they feel that you and they have points in common, then they will be open to hearing your proposal. Don't just speak it, however. Put your proposal in writing and show a willingness to change it according to their feedback. When your client can see in writing the value they will receive from you, the time it will take and the amount of money it will cost, they feel that you have operated in a completely up-front manner. Create your connection of affinity then build upon it with a match between your value proposition and their need.

Only through relationship, genuine interest and careful questioning can you finally reach the point of sale that continues to generate sales and referrals for years to come.

As I pointed out in the chapter on robot and relationship sales, you might be able to open a relationship without the level of attention to detail that I have just described. You may be able to simply lay out the benefits of your product and convince someone to purchase it. What I am suggesting to you is that you create a level of bonding and trust that allows the relationship with the person to drive the sales process. When you do this, you gain value as a human being in your life, you gain referrals over the long-term and you gain a sale with possible repeat business. In the end, taking the time to focus, be likeable and clearly present who you are and what you have to offer in light of their specific goals and needs creates affluence for you and for them. It is an affluence that rests on human community and respect.

Jack's Snack

"Visualize the entire sales call from start to finish".

Chapter 6

Accountable

Successful relationships must include two accountable parties. We sometimes find ourselves in relationships with people who are unreliable because we haven't learned the art of holding others accountable. Does that make sense? It took me quite a while to learn that when someone held me accountable for my behavior, their message was, "I think that you are capable of being an incredible person and I won't accept anything less." When I realized that my friend, wife, son or associate was actually saying to me, "I believe in you", I became much more comfortable having conversations with those around me where they held me accountable or I held them accountable for their actions. What does this kind of conversation look like? Here is a typical conversation:

"John, I'm calling to talk to you about a report that showed you were selling whole life policies in Washington State. Is this true?"

"Yes, I opened fifteen cases with unrelated individuals."

"John, we do not have a license to sell whole life policies in that state. Are you aware that you have opened this company up to liability?"

"Yes...no...I...I realize now that I did that. I'm sorry." "Let's meet with our legal team. At some point, you and I will need to talk about where we go from here. I'm sorry that this happened."

"I am too."

Sometimes holding someone accountable looks a lot like busting his or her chops but not always. Sometimes it looks like encouragement. My story below illustrates this.

Going Within:

Pauline (a.k.a. "Ma")

Pauline is my mother. She is quite possibly THE best salesperson I have ever met. Ma started selling ladies clothing when I was a kid. She moved on to selling high-end furniture, which she did for years with great success. Ma never met a stranger. The very essence of her personality was this message, I like you and believe in you! Her way of being, inspired people to be their best. She actually held the people around her accountable for their actions without being the *heavy* in any way. She never questioned my ability to achieve my full potential. Every day, her faith inspires me to be accountable to always be my best self and accountable to do what I know is right.

I haven't always held myself accountable, though. In the fall of 1978, I was employed by IBM (aka Big Blue), joining them right out of the University of Illinois, Champaign-Urbana. For those of you who know IBM, the first year for most Sales Reps and Systems Engineers, is spent in a classroom in Atlanta, GA. All new recruits make four trips there, in two to four week chunks, and we all take the same learning track, regardless of job description. And, you have to successfully pass that stage of training, or they send you home. Well, I was doing great until my third class. This is where we were "writing code", using computer languages like Basic, Cobol, APL and RPG 3.

Yikes! I sucked at programming, and unlike other areas of my life, I could not "fake it till I make it". There was no place to hide, when you turned in your programming "deck". I just did not get it, and all I really knew about computers at the time, was that they were longer than they were wide, and they cost a lot of money. How embarrassing it was, to get sent home as a failure, with one future chance to come back and finish what I started. Of course, it wasn't my fault I was so incompetent. You see, Ma was sick at the time, just having been released from a hospital after a major health scare, and my message to all: I HAD to come home, to visit my sick mother. Liar liar, pants on fire. I didn't take responsibility for failing. Rather I played the "victim" role (which I disdain today), and blamed everyone else. Ma set me straight and held me accountable for my behavior, as she should. I hated the way I felt, and I hated the lie I told myself. This was a "game-changer" for me, for the rest of my life.

The postscript: I went back to my peers on Roswell Road, and finished the course, and the rest is history.

Reaching Out:

You Can Do Better

My wife, Kemi Kim, is also one of the best salesperson I've ever known. Of course she will vehemently deny she is, and proceed to tell you how she really dislikes sales. However, if you include the words persuasive, persistent, pragmatic and influential in the definition, Kemi gets what she wants--and when she wants it. The difference between her and others like me: she kinda sneaks up on you, and disarms you along the way. Most of us recognize a *Peddler* from a mile away, and as they approach, we hold on to our wallets, for safe measure. When they finally pass, we count our fingers, just to make sure they're all still intact. You know the (sales) type, right? Kemi does naturally, what I teach Clients to do: *always assume the sale.* She knows what desired outcome she wants/needs/expects, and she assumes she's gonna get exactly what she asks for. Simple, but not easy. If you're going to say NO to Kemi Kim, you'd better have an airtight argument, because you can bet that she does!

She holds herself accountable for results, which is exactly what we should ALL do, in every aspect of our lives.

The Next Step

Do you have a sister, brother, cousin or close friend? Pick one of these types of individuals whom you know fairly well. Call them up or meet them and ask them if there is any goal in their life that you can support them in achieving. Offer to help hold them accountable for what they say they are going to do until they do it. In the meantime, stay in touch to ensure milestones are being reached and progress is being made. They'll appreciate your help down the road.

Building Blocks of Successful Sales

Accountability often looks a lot like self-discipline doesn't it? The one big difference between a successful sales pro and an unsuccessful sales pro is their willingness to carefully uncover and then overcome objections. When most people feel or hear resistance, their first inclination is to back off. Who wants to go where they're not wanted, right? Except, who says you're not wanted? Your potential customer will almost certainly stall and present objections to opening a relationship with you. This is their way of asking you to provide them with more accurate and complete information.

When you have progressed in your sales conversation to the point of opening and you encounter resistance, it is up to you to hold yourself accountable for following through to the conversation. Your brain and emotions may sabotage your efforts telling you to back off and not to be pushy. Stand firm in the knowledge that you can uncover real objections in an easy, conversational way that puts your potential customer at ease.

Most of us are smart, creative individuals. Some of us are geniuses. A genius is just so gifted at what they do that they can be successful effortlessly. For instance, a mathematical genius could easily take a math test of any level and perform well on it with little or no study. For the rest of us, advance preparation is our silver bullet. We win because we sat down and prepared to win. In sales, your silver bullet is the time you spent anticipating the kind of objections that your potential customer might have and formulating clear, accurate and convincing responses to those objections.

There are two important reasons why investing the time to anticipate objections pays off. First of all, you know the answers. You can say with confidence that fifty to sixty percent of your customers have been picked up by national affiliates under your company's representation. You can say that long and short-term projections on their industry are available and that you can incorporate them into a financial summary. Why can you make these and other responses with surety? You can because you thought ahead, did your research and confirmed your answers. The average expendable income of the individuals on your marketing database? Well, that's on average $20,000.00 a year. Why do you know this fact? You know it because you imagined that if you were this customer that is precisely what you would want to know before you spent your money on a large database. How did you know this? You had to do a little digging in the files, maybe even get some help.

That homework pays off! It shows that you are accountable for the complete and accurate presentation of your product or service.

The second payoff for preparing to overcome objections is that when you are prepared it shows! You can lean back, smile and chat with the cool confidence that you do know the answers and you are presenting them with the best option for their money. Your casual attitude allows you to continually drill down through your customer's stalls, into their objections and finally to the point of asking them for their business.

How do you pack a silver bullet? Here are six "surefire" ways. (I couldn't resist!)

- Differentiate between stalls and objections.

- Identify the real objections behind the stalls.
- Convert stalls into objections that can be overcome.
- Anticipate objections and formulate responses to each one in advance.
- Learn techniques to address objections comfortably and conversationally.
- Apply a process to conquer objections and solve problems.

Besides a horse's room in a barn, what is a stall? A stall is a statement like, *I want to think about it*, or *I have to talk with my partner*. Why are these stalls and not objections? They are stalls because, unlike objections, they cannot be overcome. A stall is a way for a potential customer to ask you to convince them more and better. They have both positive and negative feelings at this point. They are interested enough not to simply walk away but not interested enough to clearly tell you what their issue is. It's up to you to take a stall and uncover the objection behind it. It's up to you to hold yourself accountable for moving ahead even though you feel like calling it quits at this level of ambiguous resistance.

When you hear a stall, relax! You have a system to convert a stall into an objection and then dismantle the objection. Knowing that you have the tools to do this will allow you to be casual and conversational with your potential client.

What are some common stalls that you hear? In our business, we hear most frequently, *I need to talk to my (insert name of other decision-maker) first*. The first thing that I do when I hear a stall is to explore it. I become curious about it. For example, *Do you and your (d/m) usually make all of your business purchases together? For what sort of product is your partner looking?* Usually, with this sort of curious questioning, I am able to uncover an objection. Often an objection is that our future customer believes that they can get the same service from another source for less money. Once I discover that that is the real objection, I'm at liberty to offer reassurance and overcome the objection. Then I am ready to resell the product or service.

I've built up a collection of common objections, which I have written down. Next to each objection, I write down my response to overcome that objection. Usually, people are objecting to price, the product or service or the company... or you! I have researched and created clear, strong responses to these objections. When I hear a new one, I write it down and go find out how to overcome it. Having the right information does make a difference but you also have to know how to gently introduce that information so that you are not appearing argumentative.

Many people respond to empathy, that is, your ability to emotionally connect with a candidate. *I know how you feel about...* goes a long way in any relationship toward mutual agreement!

Honestly admit that your candidate customer's objection is correct and then counter it. For example, Yes, it is a lengthy deployment time. That allows us to trouble- shoot on-site instead of charging you for support calls too soon, after product launch.

Focus yourself and your customer on the *reality* of the present and the future and don't become mired down in discussions of the past. Sometimes, you can sense that the customer is uncertain. They aren't really sure one way or the other. When dealing with uncertainty, push back gently with a question such as, *Why do you believe that X is a better choice for you?*

Clarity is uppermost in any sort of communication. My favorite question, *Let me make sure I understand...........*To avoid crossed wires, always, in any relationship, restate what you heard. Once you have heard an objection, say it back to be sure that you got it right.

Just doing this says loud and clear, *I am listening to you and want to honestly respond to you.*

Once you have listened and acknowledged by restating what you've heard, make sure that that is the only objection you are facing. How do you make sure? Ask! Always ask.

Take a moment to point out how other people with the same objection eventually found that your solution was the best for them. Then ask them if they feel that you have addressed their concern. Go back to the process of opening a relationship with them and make a point of talking about the first step towards completing the purchase.

We're all human and our natural first reaction to stalls is to become defensive or argumentative. You're there to engage your customer in a team effort. The two of you are working to solve their problem in the best way possible. Make your responses positive.

I like to argue, or more accurately, debate, I admit it. When I hear a stall, my first response is to mix it up with the individual somehow. Over the years, I have learned to automatically rechannel this energy into a smile and an acknowledgment that they have a good point! Wow! (If only we could do this when we argue with our kids and spouses too!)

Accountability means putting in work before you walk through the door. *Address Concerns Early* and with anticipation and you will *ACE* the sale!

Jack's Snack:

"We are rewarded only to the extent by which we add value to those Clients we are privileged to serve".

Chapter 7

Trusting

Have you ever teamed up with someone else to accomplish a project? Initially, you meet to discuss the project and map out your tasks and deadlines.

Day-by-day, you work together to complete the project, communicating sometimes five or six times a day. Did you ever change the subject from work to a topic more personal, and share some aspect of yourself? For instance, confiding that you had tried to complete this sort of project in the past alone and found that you couldn't do it as effectively. Or perhaps sharing that you just found out that your mother has a chronic disease and you're scared. This kind of sharing infers, *I trust you as a person.* It says, *I see you as a fellow human being-- vulnerabilities and all.* There really is no other way to establish lasting relationships with people, except by trusting them. Sometimes trust takes the form of letting them make their own mistakes and trusting that they can take responsibility for whatever happens. When you find yourself struggling to "stay in control" either of your feelings or of someone else's, stop and reflect. You may be damaging an important relationship.

Going Within:

Talking to You Now

I have to confess something to you. Showing vulnerability is one of my numerous character flaws. I'm taking vulnerability lessons all the time and I will continue, until the day that I'm pushing up daisies. It has always been difficult for me to let down my guard and trust someone enough to share my real feelings with them. This is not a good thing, since relationships are all about trust and vulnerability. I now realize that I can't create the ever-increasing, deeply satisfying life that I want without learning to trust others--and trust in them--more.

Every story that I share with you in this book, is me saying to you, *I trust you. Here is how I show my confidence.* Few will trust you if you don't trust them. Yes, you may still sell them something, once or twice but that relationship will not continue to grow and expand. That person will not scatter goodwill about you in their network and your life will simply be a rubber band-- expanding briefly then collapsing to its former size. If I can learn to open my heart and mind to others despite years of resistance and "control walls," you can too.

Reaching Out:

Taking More Than Money

When my oldest son, Nick was seventeen, I wanted to teach him finance and judicious spending, I opened a bank account for him with both of our names on the signature card. Nick got a job and started making money each week, some of which he deposited into the account.

After about six months, I realized that I was still footing the bill for Nick's cell phone, car insurance and his dirt bike. He had agreed to contribute a certain amount of money for these expenses. I reminded him of this but he did not pay me. I grew more and more frustrated and decided that I would take matters into my own hands.

I went to the bank and took all of the money out myself, one thousand dollars, without telling Nick. When Nick went to the bank the next time, he was devastated to discover that I had taken all of his money. The only thing that he could say when we talked about it was, "All I know is that I had one thousand dollars and now I don't have anything."

After working to instill trust in my son, I had single- handedly damaged it by not trusting in Nick to be accountable. He was either going to pay me and pay me in a timely manner, or he was not going to pay me. Whatever Nick chose to do would be his decision. I took the opportunity for him to be held accountable away from him. I made a mistake. Nick never put another dollar in that account.

The first thing that I did was go to Nick and say, "I'm sorry that I went into your account and took the money without your knowledge. That was wrong of me and I feel bad. I'll never do that again". The second thing that I did was go down to the bank with Nick after he turned eighteen and helped him open an account in his name only. Every parent makes mistakes. I can't beat myself up about this one. I can learn from it however and hopefully, by sharing my mistake with you, you can learn from it also.

The Next Step

It's time to take inventory! Do you have a current or past relationship that is suffering or has ended because you could not admit that you were wrong? Do you have a churning in your gut when you think of certain people? Why is that? It took me a long time to realize this very important truth: Being vulnerable or admitting you're wrong, is about trust. It's about trusting the other person to respond appropriately, to listen and to forgive you. Trust makes it a little easier to acknowledge that you messed up and trust makes it a lot easier to establish lasting relationships.

What about the people closest to you? How often have to come to them and said, "I'm wrong," or "I don't know what to do?" These are uncomfortable conversations to have. Make an appointment to sit down with a colleague, friend or family member and acknowledge to them that you made a mistake in some way, that you are sorry and that you want to know how to make it right.

When you've completed this conversation, send me an e-mail at jack@lifesasalescall.com and tell me how it went. I want to learn from you!

Building Blocks of Successful Sales

Deep down, whether we admit it or not, many of us feel that the second part of the equation in relationship sales is not an honest part of the relationship. What I mean is that when you have engaged with another person, opened up to them and trusted them, been accountable and respectful. .. How are you then going to turn around and ask them for their business? Deep down, doesn't that feel a little bit disingenuous to you?

I'm here to tell you that that is not true.

What is true is that you are asking a question. You are asking this individual if they would like to buy your product or service based on the value of the product and their level of investment in it. You are not asking them for a favor, you are asking them if your value equation makes sense. Your friendship/relationship does not depend on this sale. That depends on you and them. Ideally, you would continue to have a relationship of some kind regardless of whether or not they chose to buy from you at that moment. We'll talk about this later in this chapter. For now, I want you to focus on the discomfort that you might feel when it comes time to ask a friend for their business.

Another reason you may feel uncomfortable in asking for a sale has to do with trust. When you ask someone for their business, you are making yourself vulnerable to them. Some would say that you are openly courting rejection. Keep in mind that you are not your product or service. You are you and if they don't want to buy from you, well, they may change their mind later. In the meantime, you as an individual have a lot to offer anyone. Why? You have a lot to offer because you know how to create and maintain a relationship and that is a most valuable skill.

When you ask someone if they would be interested in purchasing from you, you are simply asking a question. You are inquiring as to their state of mind at that moment. Up to now, you have hopefully listened to their stalls, drilled down to their objections and overcome them.

Here are some signs that your candidate is ready to become your customer. They:

1. Express a strong interest verbally in your solution (I like the way that this works!)
2. Step into the customer role directly (What do you see as our most profitable application?)
3. Provides positive, unsoliticited feedback (I have really enjoyed meeting you and learning about this).
4. Show positive body language (leaning forward, smiling, open arms etc.).

When you identify that your friend wants to become your customer, then you are ready to ask for their business or open the sales relationship.

Knowing the right way to open is an art. Like all facets of relationships and of selling, opening calls for careful listening and analysis on your part. Ask yourself "What kind of opening is best for the situation and personality type with which I am dealing?"

The most popular and successful way of opening is to summarize the benefits that you have just presented to the individual. For example, "The site allows you access to over sixty thousand potential customers. You agree that the price is a small investment for the value you can receive from being a member of this site. Can I begin the process of making you a member now?"

Often, our potential customer is very busy and doesn't have time to talk with us. Nevertheless, they have expressed a strong interest and shown other signs that they are ready to buy. If this is the case, simply be direct and ask, "I know that you're busy. Can we sit down and sign a contract now?"

Some people are hard to read, they may not be very expressive or they tend to be cautious. In this case, gradually or indirectly leading up to the opening may work best for you. Here is an indirect open that I used recently:

"How many product lines do you currently have?"

"How many sales professionals are representing those products for you?"

"Do you currently have a sales training program in place?"

"Are you clear on how vital it is to have well-trained people in your sales department?"

"Would you agree that the NextStep Solutions sales training program is ideally suited to your company's needs and delivers a great return on your investment?"

No matter where you are in the sales process, continually recall that this individual is looking for a value that exceeds their investment. They are not looking for a value that equals their investment--they want the value to exceed their investment. They want a DEAL!

We've all seen salesmen on TV who simply assume that the customer is buying their product or service. "I'll wrap that right up for you!"or "What time do you want to me come by?" Certainly, if you are comfortable with the individual and your sense is that they have already tacitly agreed to the purchase, and then use an assumptive opening. I would caution you against using this unless you are very secure in the customer's intention. The last thing you want to do in any relationship is to be controlling or pushy. If they don't want to buy your product, that is their choice. Be confident that they will buy next time.

Similar to the assumptive opening is the alternate choice opening. Here, again, you are assuming that the customer is ready to buy. You present them with an either/or choice that signals their decision. For instance, "Shall I write you down for Saturday or would you prefer Monday?" "Would you like that shipped next day or in three to four days?"

In this way, you are opening the door and instead of asking them to come in, you're asking them which chair they would like to sit in. You are sure that they want to come in.

Benjamin Franklin was an astute judge of character and he was a wily salesman himself. One opening in which you "weigh" the pros and cons of the decision is named after him: The Benjamin Franklin Open. In this scenario, you sit down and write or list out loud to the potential customer all of the pros. When it comes time to list the cons, stay silent and let the other person supply these. Usually, at this point, they realize that you have overcome their objections and they are willing to buy.

Allow me to introduce you to the Puppy Dog open. (Let me digress. Say you have young kids at home. Your neighbor comes over with a puppy and says, "Just keep her for thirty days and if your children don't just absolutely fall in love... Do you think that he'll ever get that puppy back? I don't think so!)

Allow your client to try your product for a specified period of time before they buy it. This usually results in opening a sale if you have determined that the client has a real need for the product and sees it as a high value for their investment.

Regardless of which open you chose to use, remember to persistently ask for their business. Persistence is a major part of your success. More than fifty percent of sales pros give up after the first "No." Trust the process and trust me when I tell you that simply continuing to ask for their business up to and beyond fifteen times.

This is what I call the Rule of Fifteen. Research supports the premise that if you find a way to ask for one's business, fifteen times or more, there's an eighty percent chance that they'll open a relationship with you, on some level. Persistence is rewarded.

The odds of you opening a relationship actually increase dramatically after the third "no."That's right! You have an eighty percent chance of opening a sale if you ask for their business fifteen times or more over time, even if the sale is a small "yes" relatively speaking.

Even though you have completed a sale with a client, you are actually just beginning that relationship with that person. That's why I call it opening instead of closing. Think of sales as a band of gold that grows thicker and thicker. It is a circle that continues on and on, not a line with a beginning and an end.

Articulate your client's long-term concerns to them and provide them with long-term solutions. Not only are you building a relationship you are also building future sales. *Life's a Sales Call!* There's no need to separate the two as long as you are being authentic in your relation- ships and as long as the client feels that they are getting value from their investment.

Jack's Snack

"When the student is ready, the teacher appears".

Chapter 8

Inspirational

Have you ever had the experience of seeing a new world? It could take the form of learning to scuba dive, visiting Peru, listening to your intuition for the first time or learning physics. Inspiring someone is the act of introducing them to a new world. I have found that all around me there are people needing inspiration. People are asking me to show them a new world. Their requests take different forms. For example, a receptionist may confide in me that her daughter wants to go to college. I may say to her that the girl needs to meet with her high school counselor as well as with a college financial aid counselor. For me, this knowledge is part of my world. For her, this advice gives her the way to move toward a new future. The next step may be a mystery to someone in your life and you could be the person who holds the key. I'm not offering unsolicited advice. I recommend generously offering what you have to those who ask for help.

Going Within:

The World of Mathematics

I knew I needed help and I wasn't sure where I would find it. When I turned seventeen, I began to take advanced level courses in high school. I was under a lot of pressure to compete for entrance into a good college. Until then, I had been a straight A student, but now my consecutive string of A grades was being challenged as I found myself in over my head. Due to the complexity of the material, my parents couldn't really assist me.

Our next-door neighbor, growing up, Steve or Dr. Steve Cerefice worked at AMOCO Oil Company (now British Petroleum or BP). He had three young boys, at the time. I asked Steve for help with my math and science homework. His response was to clear the table after supper two or three nights a week and spend hours with me, helping me to complete my homework for over a year. I am forever grateful to Steve, not only for enabling me to maintain my A average and gain admittance to the University of Illinois, but also for opening up to me, the world of mathematics. He inspired me to give freely to others with no expectation of payback. Today, what a great day it is, when you can do a favor for someone with little or no hope of a payback!

Reaching Out:

Speak for Yourself!

One day I got a call from a young man named Ray Hollister. Ray had a wife and four children at the time. He was changing careers and wanted to be a professional speaker. Ray had developed a patented system, to aid students in studying for tests and he wanted to travel around the country sharing this method. The problem was he didn't know a thing about the speaking industry.

I invited Ray to my house in the summer of '92. Ray was inspired by where we lived and he had a hard time believing that he too could someday own a nice home.

Remembering the inspiration I had received from Dr. Cerefice, I began to listen to Ray's presentations and critique them several times a week. I encouraged him and shared all of the knowledge that I had amassed about the speaking industry. I worked to help him find a job where he could gain experience speaking. I let him know that he could become successful beyond his wildest imagination, if that was his goal and focus.

Ultimately, Ray moved to the Pacific Northwest where he did experience success with his career.

A decade passed without any contact between us. Then, one day, I googled my own name, just out of uriosity. Ray Hollister's name showed up in a magazine interview saying that the number one person that had inspired him was Jack Warkenthien. Wow!

The Next Step

You know what you have to offer. In your business, your mastermind group or other professional organizations, begin to watch for people whom you might mentor or be of service. They are out there looking for you. You have the experience and the knowledge to guide them toward their goals and to inspire them.

Remember, you are developing points of common interest with everyone that you meet. Be open to the possibility that one of these people may need you as a mentor or guide. Make yourself available, be curious, be patient and see what happens. Write and tell me about it, as I'd like to know!
jack@lifesasalescall.com

Building Blocks to Successful Sales

The ability to inspire others cannot be overrated. Inspiration is the heart and soul of commerce. Without it, we'd all be walking a treadmill devoid of possibilities and positive changes. Even if you sell asbestos cleanup services, you must still inspire your customers enough that they willingly offer you referrals. If you're like many other enterprises, up to eighty percent of your business may be sourced from referrals.

If you're in sales, I'm sure you've heard this before ...blah, blah, blah. Let me put it a different way: When you inspire your clients, they are inspired to talk about you to their friends easily and frequently.

You can inspire a client simply by being a good listener. Train yourself to listen at least seventy-five percent of the time and limit your talking to only twenty-five percent. Keep your eyes focused on them, really listen and then repeat back what you heard. Keep your mind moving toward long-term solutions. Encourage your client to open up about past mistakes, vendors and goals with curious, genuine questions. I can't stress listening enough. Not only in sales but also in every relationship in your life, even if it's your relationship with the guy at the Starbucks counter. Practice asking questions and then shutting up. You may wake up in six months time to discover that you have quadrupled your friends, inspired your significant only and elicited confidence from your children. Did I leave something out? Oh yeah, increase your sales! Few things inspire people more than being really listened to.

Excellent service goes a long way. These days, many business people are from that group known as Generation X. They were born between 1964 and 1971 and they have a particular set of characteristics, not the least of which is the desire to have everything done accurately and quickly. All customers appreciate immediate response and accurate information, but this group demands it. Use the Internet to your advantage. The same goes for phone calls. Double-check the information that you give out. If mortgage rates are hovering around four percent today, that doesn't mean that's where they will be tomorrow morning. Check and check again. Use the internet as a convenient library and research assistant.

A tangible thank you for your business, often minimizes buyer's remorse. Since buyer's remorse usually occurs on the first day that they receive your product, make sure that you accompany a delivery with a gift and a personal thank you by phone and in writing.

Some people like to send cards and plants. These are good ideas. Also, consider finding out up front what their favorite restaurant, candy, wine etc. is. A gift that is so personal makes an impression and continues to make an impression throughout the life of your relationship. One sales person I know noticed that the client had a very busy staff. The sales pro found the restaurant where the staff liked to congregate nearby and purchased a gift certificate for drinks and appetizers. Talk about a splash! The client enjoyed the gift and really appreciated the gesture towards her staff. This was a great first step towards a long relationship.

I frequently share my "Four Laws of Referability."Do you want people to crusade on your behalf? Are you interested in referrals? Then, I suggest that you follow the *four* suggestions below:

1. ***Do what you say you're going to do.*** Did you say that you would send a report by next week? Don't do it the week after that. Deliver on your promise. I wouldn't trust someone who said one thing and did another. The slightest inconsistency on your part in this area spells disaster. Did you say that the fixed price was $ and then you added on a twenty percent fee? Kiss that relationship goodbye! You would have been better off to simply give them a higher price or express in writing that the price is subject to change without notice.

    Juanell Teague, a dear friend and coach to many professional speakers, including me, has a mantra, "Tell the truth, quicker and faster." Telling the truth means stating the details and it means actually doing what you said you were going to do within the confines of your commitments.

2. ***Finish what you start.*** Nothing feels better to a client than knowing that you are going to do what you say you are going to do, completely. The first thing out of their mouth when referring you to someone else will be, "Jack always makes sure that I am completely satisfied and everything is finished. And he's fast and accurate too!"

    If you and a client meet and discuss ideas, make sure that each idea is explored thoroughly. Do your research and do your follow-up with him or her. Just because it wasn't your idea, or it may occur six months from now is no reason not to complete the job of marking out goals and exploring them.

When you open a relationship with a client, and they purchase your product or service, be sure to continue to maintain the relationship (I'll talk more about this in the next chapter).

Installing a security system but not working with the technicians to iron out the kinks is doing the job halfway. Your job is to make your client happy.

3. **Be on time.** In my opinion, being on time means five minutes early, not fifteen minutes early. Being that early shows that you lack time management. Being on time also means not being five minutes late. Late is late.

    You and I both know that time is money. We also know that trust is the fulcrum of relationships. When you disregard these two principles by not showing up when you said you were going to show up, you are losing money and degrading relationship. I had a physician who made me wait ten minutes or more for every appointment. I learned more about how I often glossed over the actions of others that felt disrespectful to me. I also realized that I was losing precious time sitting in the reception area. As this realization dawned on me, I asked my doctor why each time we were to meet I had to wait for at least twenty minutes.

    We both learned from that experience and as long as I used that physician, he assured me that I'd have minimal waiting times. You may think that it's strange for a professional to have to be reminded of such a simple idea, but look at yourself. You are, no doubt, a competent individual who excells at what you do. Yet, holding to all of the strings and strands of the day and the relationships in that day can sometimes lead to slippage. Everyone finds that they can't be on time one hundred percent of the time. I am talking about the person who is chronically unaccountable to themselves and to those people who trust them.

4. ***Say Please and Thank You.*** This simple request works on and off the business field. Imagine the power of preceding every request with a "Please" and following every favor with "Thank you."It's simple, but not easy. How few people we meet in the course of our daily routine actually remember to express gratitude, on some level?

   Why am I telling you this? I'm telling you this because acknowledgement cannot be minimized or trivialized, EVER. How do we acknowledge? The simplest words such as please and thank you have the greatest effect, especially if they are spoken sincerely and often.

   Sometimes we say thank you with a note as well. People like to be treated as if they are important to you and when you show them respect and kindness in your manner and speech, they respond with openness.

Jack's Snack:

"Obstacles are those frightful things you see, when you take your eyes off your goal".

Chapter 9

Observant

If you believe like I do that *Life's A Sales Call*, then you know that everything going on around you in life is part of that sales call. When you are sitting in a cafe reading the paper, who is sitting around you? What is playing on the sound system? As you enter a room full of people, who is standing in a group and who is not?

What sort of conversations are these people having? Are there individuals who keep coming and going? Is there a slight commotion down the hall? Do you see anyone that you recognize from another context?

Who does everyone seem to know? Observing the details around you can greatly enhance your ability to make connections with other people. The late, great Yogi Berra was famous for saying, "It's amazing what you can see if you just watch people". Pay attention and you may learn something about someone that allows you to be his or her friend. You may learn something about someone that changes and inspires you. You may discover a hidden truth that dramatically affects a business decision. In the event of a fire, we're taught to stop, drop and roll. In the important activity of observing: Watch, listen and learn.

Going Within:

The Real McCoy

A while back, I was waiting in line at Love Field in Dallas when Herb Kelleher walked by. Herb Kelleher is the Chairman Emeritus and co-founder of Southwest Airlines. Since I had met Herb once, I stepped out of line to say hello. Though I doubt that he actually remembered me, he responded in a genuinely friendly way. I guessed that Herb was on my flight back to San Antonio, so I made sure that I sat in front, in case there was a chance of a conversation.

Herb did get on the plane and immediately began helping a flight attendant stow some luggage. He then began to assist the crew with whatever they needed, passing out coffee and tea or snacks. I watched Herb's behavior carefully and realized that he is who he represents himself to be. He is not an arrogant, condescending executive. He's a warm human being who believes in teamwork. I watched as he hugged the flight attendants and then I managed to get my picture taken with Herb.

By being observant, I not only met a role model and inspiration, I also got a tangible keepsake of that moment.

Reaching Out:

Watching the Fire

My friend Randall was staying in a hotel in New York for a week. He told me this story. He said, "The hotel had a nice, comfortable lobby with big chairs and a fireplace. Each day, as I left the hotel in the morning and then returned in the evening, I noticed the same person sitting in a chair in front of the fire. He was somewhere between eighty and one hundred and twenty years old. He was dressed in drab colors and his hair was white. He sat straight in the chair and stared at the fire. I didn't know if he was a guest in the hotel or a visitor. All of the rooms had fireplaces in them. I noticed that he looked sad."

"On the third day, I sat down across from the elderly gentleman and began to talk idly about the comforts of a fire in winter. He looked away from the fire and into my eyes and I saw the bright, steely eyes of a highly aware individual. His eyes also had a tinge of grief in them. As we talked, his story unraveled. As a young man, this fellow had been a soldier in World War II. His entire unit was assigned a parachute mission. The fighter plane was to fly them over enemy territory and drop them down to assist ground troops. This man and all of his buddies boarded the plane. At the end of the day, the only man survived was my new friend. He spent that night in an empty barracks. Unable to bear the silence, he took his blankets and built a fire and slept outside in the cold that night. Each year, on the anniversary of that doomed flight, he sits and stares into the fire, remembering his buddies one by one.

I was saddened and fascinated by the old man's tale. After he finished speaking, I thanked him for sharing his story with me. I told him that I had noticed him and had wondered why he stared at the fire so long. He straightened up in his chair and smiled at me and shook my hand. 'Tell me about yourself,' he said, and I got the feeling that I was in the company of a man used to commanding others. I told him that I was a salesman for an Italian tile manufacturer as well as other specialty building supplies. I told him about my wife and kids and where I was from originally. After awhile, he thanked me for listening, took my card and wished me a nice stay in the city. I left feeling warmed by the contact with another human being. I was so glad that I had paid attention to the people around me as I came and went on my own business."

"About two weeks later, I received a call from the purchasing agent for a string of luxury hotels. She wanted to review the tiles I had to offer with an interest in tiling over a million square feet! Eventually, I asked her how she got my name and number and she told me that the owner of the hotel chain had given it to her. It had to be the man I had watched; I confirmed with her that the owner was an octogenarian man with snow white hair."

Not every point of observation is going to result in the biggest sale of your life. **Life's a Sales Call!** When you walk through it, pay attention. You'll never know what you missed.

The Next Step

I want you to start a diary of conversations you have with clients every day. Use a spiral- bound, college-ruled notebook to take notes. After you have parted company, I want you to make detailed notes about the conversation. For instance, was there any point in the conversation when the individual moved from answering your questions in brief, polite statements and began to light up and speak excitedly? What prompted this change? Did you notice? Keep this diary for at least a month. You may decide to always keep one. Why? Keenly observing each person whom you meet and the nuances of your conversation allows you to maintain an extremely customized and personable relationship with them. The note, "Lit up at the mention of a camping trip." Can lead you to open a conversation with, "Been camping lately?" It guides you towards sending your client notices of upcoming wilderness survival demonstrations or links to little-known state parks.

I'm curious to know how your diary experience worked for you. E-mail me at jack@lifesasalescall.com and tell me how your keen observations and curiosity affected your sales call. I want to know!

Building Blocks to Successful Sales

If you have ever been married, or even in a serious romantic relationship, you know that there comes a certain point (sometimes pretty early on) when all of your romantic gestures had better have a personal touch. For instance, if you think to bring her flowers, stop! What are her favorite flowers? What are his favorite kind of chocolate candies? Did you pay attention when she led you through the flower shop pointing out her favorites? It gets trickier. Eventually, personalized gestures are all women want and men like them too. A blue bottle with a daisy in it to remind her of your first date, a picnic, when you presented her with the same sort of bottle with a daisy. You get the picture. It is difficult to stay in a relationship with another person if you are not observing that person and if you do not work to maintain the relationship.

When it comes to sales and life, a maintenance policy is the way to go. I call it a maintenance policy because this has to be your mode of operations all the time. I'm talking 24/7. Let your maintenance policy become an automatic thing. When you see a newspaper or a magazine, have in mind two or three subjects that would interest a client or two. We'll talk about this more later.

When you start your day, plan to invest time "touching" your existing clients. This is what I call a maintenance policy. Reach out, make contact and do it in a personal way, a way that says, "I'm paying attention."As you do this, you will discover that your client has needs and wants that you didn't know about. Creating the opportunity to cross-sell and up-sell existing clients is an extremely efficient use of your time. It is six times easier to sell additional products to existing clients than it is to find new clients to sell to. Think about how you can upgrade the services or products that you now have to offer.

As your relationship with your client deepens, they become an extension of your sales force. You have shown your loyalty to them and they return the favor with referrals.

This isn't pie in the sky. This is, in fact, how the mechanism of relationships work.

Ask anyone who is married and they will tell you that it is a lot of work and it's worth it. Paying attention and maintaining the relationship is work that can be fun and rewarding if you realize that you're enriching your life, enjoying your work and making money all at the same time. In the next chapter, I will give you specific ways that you can be nurturing toward your client relationships. At this point, I think that it's important for you to commit to maintenance. Without it, all of the sincerity, trust and respect will become a memory in the mind of your client, not an enriching, ongoing relationship.

Jack's Snack:

"The Platinum Rule of Sales: Do unto others as they want you to do, unto them".

Chapter 10

Nurturing

If *life's a sales call* and sales is about relationships, then nurturing is the chocolate ice cream. What I mean is that nurturing is the sweet stuff, the reward.

A relationship of any kind is a process, not an event. A relationship is a continuum -a never ending wave. Once it begins, nurturing begins. Whether it's a potential client, an old friend, your spouse or child, nurturing the relationship grows it. What is nurturing? In a nutshell, nurturing is giving. It is giving value, things, recognition, entertainment and gifts. Some relationships gain traction over time and others fizzle out. The difference is the level of nurturing being exchanged in those relationships.

I began to realize a while back that nurturing equals time. My idea that I could race through the day focusing on "closing deals" was a mistake. Eventually, I learned to make time to just sit and listen to those that I love and those that I wish to keep in my life. Schedules are made to be flexed!

Going Within:

Feeding the Stream

My wife, Kemi loves loving. In fact, she's far more demonstrative than I, though I remind her I love her just as much. I just show it in different ways. On the fortunate days when I can work out of our home office, nary an hour goes by, where she doesn't come into my space, and nuzzle me like a cat, scratch my head (OK. I know it sounds kinda wierd, but I enjoy my scalp being scratched--must be my thinning hair line), or just tell me she loves me. This sounds terrible, but I occasionally act as if she's a distraction, especially if "I'm in the zone", an expression I use, when I'm all business. That's terribly selfish of me, I admit, and I try to catch myself before I act out. When she claims to love me more than I love her, I always counter with the same logic, "No you don't. I know for sure, cuz I measured with our yardstick, and we love each other EXACTLY the same amount".

Nurture your relationships, and they'll continue to deepen and prosper over time.

Reaching Out:

Wake up! Its Three a.m.

Nobody likes a break in routine more than children. My three sons are no exception. One year, the Cubs opened their season against the New York Mets in Japan. The game was scheduled to air at three o'clock in the morning, C.S.T. I decided to make it a big deal for the boys. I talked it up for a week. We ran out to Blockbuster (I'm dating myself) to stock up on popcorn and candy and had them running around in circles they were so excited about watching the game. At three in the morning, I went upstairs and woke them up. There we all were, in front of our TV, having a party! I know that my boys will always remember that experience and I'm so glad that I took the time to focus on nurturing them. It's not a focus I can afford to lose. If you' re reading this and you realize that you have not been nurturing the relationships in your life, start now! You've heard that phrase, "It's never too late to start." Well, that's not exactly true. When it comes to relationships, the failure to nurture can cause the relationship to die. Losing a relationship is a tragedy.

The Next Step

This week, make a practice every day of nurturing one person outside of a family member. This may mean taking someone out to lunch and just listening. It may mean sending a card, leaving a caring phone message or just asking what you can do for them that day.

Next week follow the same practice each day with your closest friends and family members, a different person each day.

Every day for a week take fifteen minutes and do something you really like to do. Go eat ice cream, shoot baskets or get a manicure. Do something just for you every day!

Building Blocks to Successful Sales

You are tuned into you. You know when you need a break and you take it. You know better than to ignore your interests, so you manage to commit to yourself. In doing so, your energy for others increases exponentially! It has to because you have got to move away from the chase and into the nurturing maintenance role every single day. Here are some ways that I have found to nurture and maintain existing client relationships:

- Stay in touch frequently, without trying to sell anything.
- Continue to inform clients of new products and services.
- Give "gifts" to your clients in the form of free education/information, entertainment/ inspiration.
- Be genuinely curious. There is still so much for you to learn about your client and their business.
- Send your clients referrals for their services.
- Become a crusader for your client's firm.

How do you stay in touch without selling? For most people that's not a problem. For sales people it often is. Your client has a wide variety of personal and business interests. Be on the lookout in the media, in conversations and in doing your own research for topics of interest to them. I like to send notes to clients. This may be an article I found, an anniversary card (of our first meeting), a birthday card or, the best gift of all, a warm introduction to a future Client.

Of course, you can always just call and say, "How are you doing?" Then, sit back and listen and be curious. Did I mention how important listening is? Sometimes late at night I will call clients' offices and leave warm, thinking-of-you messages. Those that can, call me back, those that can't let me know later how much they appreciate just hearing from me. If the Houston Rockets, Texans or Astros are playing and I can scare up a ticket or two, I like to send them my client's way. Whatever I do, whether its finding a pound of amaretto coffee that I know they like or passing on a link to a site, I am staying in touch once a month. I call it my "Touch-Twelve" system. You can become very creative with the Internet, sending newsletters, cards and notices. I prefer to rely most heavily on those kinds of contact that convey my presence such as lunches, breakfasts, phone calls, cards, topical information, jokes and small gifts. Each client has a "touchdown" day on my monthly calendar.

When you are selling services and products, it's hard to remember to update everyone about what is new in your line. People love new stuff. What's new? There is no better way to stay in touch than to just let your clients know when you can offer them more or better products. If you've done your homework and really developed a relationship with them, then when you let them know of another offer, they will be eager to learn more.

Do you occasionally provide teleclasses or real classes to people interested in learning more about your products or services? When you're considering what sort of gift to give to a client, consider crafting an informative class and offering it for free. You may sell Italian tile like my friend, Randall, and you know a lot about how to transform a room or a house with tile. That's pretty interesting. I teach people how to sell. I could offer a free class on many subjects and I have. One of my clients mentioned to me in passing that she and her husband would like to learn

Tai 'Chi (I thought that was a tea drink served in Starbucks) before they go to China on a visit. I was flipping through a local magazine and I saw that a martial arts instructor was offering three free classes for beginners. I copied down the information and e-mailed it to her that day. Another client has a daughter who wants to study art in a small private college in California, but she doesn't know a lot about those schools. I have another client who does recruiting for California colleges. I put these two together. It was easy, they really appreciated it and I felt like a million bucks! I forgot to mention that when you stay in touch each month with each client, it feels great!

I gave this advice to a colleague of mine, "Stay curious. There's always something new to learn about your clients."Feeling discouraged, he methodically called one of his clients, a boat manufacturer, on his cell phone. When his client answered, my colleague distinctly heard sheep baaing in the background. "Are those sheep I hear?" he asked.

"Yep. We offer all sorts of upholstery and I came out here personally to pick out the right hides for a special order."

My client was flabbergasted. He had no idea that his client's business extended as far as animal pelts. What else was there that he didn't know? Keeping that experience in mind, he remains genuinely curious, always looking for that surprising fact that expands his understanding of his client's needs and wants.

Referrals are beautiful, referrals are fine. While you're out there selling your wares, remember that your client is selling their wares too. I like to send at least one referral a year to each of my clients, more if I can. Is your client a banker? Perhaps you have a friend who is relocating his business to your city and needs a new bank. Does your client run a catering business? Every wedding, bar mitzvah etc. mention that crosses your path should be accompanied by an offer of this client's information with your endorsement.

Talk about showing the love! Talk about paying attention! Nothing says, "I value you," more than a referral.

Just as you hope that your client will appreciate your services and products so much that they become an extension of your sales force, so do they hope that you will be a crusader for their firm. When I say crusader I mean someone whose interest is really personal and who cares about the firm with a kind of ownership that comes from friendship and loyalty.

In fact, I suggest that you invest time in not only nurturing your Centers of Influence (a.k.a. crusaders), but also training them in the fine art of selling your firm's solutions.

Talk about sales leverage! I love S.W.I.S.S. money - *Sales While I Sleep Soundly*. That's the kind you'll generate when you invest in your crusaders. They'll be selling you when you least expect it-- and mostly without your involvement!

How many persons of influence have you known who solicit you for assistance and then neglect to tell all of their friends and colleagues about how wonderful you are? It's a cold feeling. Make a fire that burns brightly by speaking highly of your client's business whenever it could help them.

Martin Luther King, Jr. said, "In the end, we will remember not the words of our enemies, but the silence of our friends."Word-of-mouth can make or break a business. Let your word be one that makes business for your client.

Jack's Snack:

"Rich is not what you have, but who you are".

Chapter 11

Sincere

It can be difficult sometimes to tell the difference between sincerity and honesty. This is my definition of sincerity: the willingness to think about the other person rather than oneself during an interaction. It sounds simple doesn't it? Yet, how often do we find ourselves waiting for someone to stop speaking so that we can say something? Often, in that pause when they have finished speaking, a silence or an acknowledgement of what they have said can create a strong impression of sincerity.

I'm updating this book, *Life's A Sales Call!*, because I realized that how I am in my personal relationships directly affects the kind of people who are attracted to me in my business relationships. The more sincere I am with my existing friends, family and colleagues, the more I will attract people of character and content. Nothing occurs in a vacuum.

The way I am, is the way I am, regardless of whether it's in my own kitchen or in a corporate board- room. Fortunately, or unfortunately, in my business of teaching sales, I have to demonstrate my product all day, every day, when I'm out in public. I am never off the clock.

Going Within:

Let Me Impress You

I've often joked that there's nothing better than a sincere compliment, delivered to your significant only--and the operant word is *sincere*. And if you can fake that, you have it made (just kidding!). In reality, Kemi and I tend to love on each other, frequently, though I'm still not totally comfortable with PDA (public displays of affection). She's mostly the initiator of ppo-ppo (Korean for a kiss), and of course I reciprocate. However, Kemi knows when it's just a rote response to her advances, or whether I'm sincerely returning her show of love and affection. We exchange a lot of funny words and phrases that are uniquely ours, and it happens to be our language of love.

If you can't be sincere in your efforts with those you love, how can you be true to those that don't know you as well?

I'll never forget what my mother said to me one day, "The quality of your life is measured by the quality of your relationships."When I can maintain sincerity in my most private relationships, then that cohesiveness shines through in me and I find people approaching me, instinctively wanting to do business with a sincere person.

Reaching Out:

Working the Room

After years and years of practice in developing my sales skills, I know how to make one hundred friends in twenty-four hours. I am motivated to remember people's names and details about them. I can carry on a conversation with anyone and/or I can entertain an entire group. This skill at being sincere in the short-term has helped me open many a deal. It's never far from my mind however that the ability to keep these customers and have them refer me to others has more to do with my sincerity in the long term.

The Next Step

I'm sure that you have some sort of networking activity planned in the next couple of weeks, so let's start with that. As you use your skills to connect to other people and determine their needs, make it a practice to repeat back to the other person what you heard about them. Who is this person? What are they passionate about? What have they invested themselves in? Don't stop at finding out that they have a need for your product or services. In a relaxed and focused way, communicate to at least two people that you are actually interested in them. The next day, follow up your conversation with a "touch" that speaks to them as individuals. Find "non- sales" reasons to stay in touch with your clients. I recommend my Touch-Twelve system that allows you to make a significant contact with your top Centers of Influence (COIs) each month. Whether you are *informing, educating , entertaining or recognizing* them, make sure that you focus your attention on them monthly. Using your observation skills, you should have a wealth of information about their passions, goals and dreams to communicate your personal interest in them effectively.

At the end of four months, take inventory of these relationships. Do they feel solid and alive? Are your relationships growing in depth? Are they reciprocal? Will they lead to new business? Send me an e-mail and let me know the outcome at jack@lifesasalescall.com .

Building Blocks to Successful Sales

I'll bet that you're wondering right now where your sincerity ranks on a scale of one to ten. An easy gauge of our sincerity level with others is an assessment of our COIs.

A center of influence is a person with whom you have a deep relationship and who is influential more than persuasive-- someone who is significant, and not just successful.

Now is the time to make a list of these individuals. If the list is short, you are not alone. We are all constantly learning and improving our relationship skills. I couldn't have written this book if I didn't visit the list on a regular basis. Let's take inventory. Whether you have five or twenty-five COIs, you will cultivate those relationships with great attention to the details that we've discussed so far, especially with a maintenance plan with no reciprocal expectations.

Ideally, each person in your trade area who trusts and respects you and your work is a hub in a wheel of influence that reaches to many people. Sincerely nurturing existing relationships is one of the most effective forms of developing new business. Let's take a look at some of the advantages of working with your COIs.

1. When you can contact a corporate decision-maker directly, based on a mutual friendship, you can avoid the red tape and difficult gate-keeping that can occur in a large company.

2. Having access to someone is one thing, having that

116

person emotionally ready to hear what you have to say is another thing altogether. When you are a trusted friend of a trusted friend, then their minds and ears are truly open to what you have to say.

3. Your COIs really understand what a great value you are to them and to any business. You don't have to sell them on you. They are happy to help in most cases, saving you much time and effort.

4. Nothing oils a friendship and makes it hum more than allowing one person to be helpful to another. We all like to feel that we are helpful to our friends. Give, by receiving, from your COIs.

5. When you work with their friends and colleagues, your COIs will be reminded what a great value you are and they are likely to further engage you as well.

In summary, developing your business through your COIs is a cost-effective way to create more business. Keep in mind: sincerity should be the core of all of your interactions. If you are honestly engaging people as a concerned human being, then they will know that and they will respond openly to your request for names of colleagues in the field to contact. If, however, you have not really had a genuine concern for this person, but rather for your own welfare, they will see right through you. Sincerity with centers of influence is the key that opens other doors.

Among your COIs who do you think has the widest reach to the greatest opportunities? Have you been maintaining that relationship on a regular basis? If you realize that you have not been vigilant in maintaining your COI relationships, now is the time to start! You will need to wait months to try mining those relationships.

Everything happens in the perfect time, so if you are not ready, methodically work toward the day when you are. You will know when it's time to try the key in the lock.

Let's say that you have enough COIs that you feel are strong and you decide to ask them for contact names. Before you make that call, take a minute to think about their relationship with you. What are they getting out of it? How would this individual see you? What strengths do you think they see in you? What weaknesses do they see? Why do they like you?

Can you think of a specific person or organization to which you would like this COI to introduce you? Have the name or names in mind so that you can make your request as specific as possible. The more specific the request, the easier it is for your COI to grant it or understand a viable option to it.

You still have quite a few more preparation steps before you pick up that phone. Going methodically through this process will ensure its success, so relax and be confident that when you actually do begin to develop your COIs you will reap the rewards of your careful preparation.

I like to come up with a way to thank my COI before I even ask them for a favor. What is their favorite restaurant? What is their favorite team? Be creative in your thank you; that's part of maintaining the relationship.

O.K., now you're ready to have a conversation with your COIs. What sort of information about a contact or referred parties would be the most helpful? Off the top of your head you could probably come up with these:

1. *How do you know this person?*
2. *How long have you known each other?*
3. *Tell me about his or her business.*
4. *How would you describe the candidate's personality?*
5. *How do you think I can help the candidate?*
6. Finally, ask them, "What can I do for you?" Whatever you may have in mind to thank them can only be improved upon by their own suggestion. Always remember their favorite radio station: WII/FM, or what's in it for ME?

Once you've gathered this information from your COI, you're ready to call the referred party and present yourself to them. This can be a little bit tricky. After all, your primary goal is to establish an easy, familiarity with the person. In a short period of time, you will need to convey trust, likeability and respect. It doesn't hurt for you to write down a possible outline to use. The more prepared you are, the more relaxed and normal you will feel in asking this person for their business.

One possible template includes telling the candidate who you are and where you work. Mention your mutual friend and talk a little bit about how you and the COIs know one another. Hint at a benefit by explaining that the COI had found so much value in the product or service that you represent that they referred me to you, thinking that you might be interested in this value as well. Now, you have the opportunity to ask if the product or service they are currently using is meeting their needs. Be curious and low-keyed. Remember that you are a team with your clients, each of you working to find them the best solutions. Hopefully that solution will include you. Be open to the possibility that the solution may not be you and be prepared to be helpful in any way that you can be. Since your main emphasis is on a relationship rather than a sale, you can really focus on the individual. Finally, setup a time to meet! Your only sale at this time should be an appointment, if the referred party is qualified and interested.

Take your time to identify, prepare and contact your COIs. As you work your way down the list with a positive sense of connecting to strong relationships in your life, you will gradually cultivate an ever-widening scope of influence for yourself.

Jack's Snack:

"Identify your most frequently heard objections, and then overcome them in advance. Build a collection of these and create your own Sales Playbook".

Chapter 12

Honest

How is being honest different from having integrity? I had to ask myself that question as I was writing this book. For me, honesty is telling the truth when it needs to be told. It is a component of integrity. Integrity to me is creating a life that is aligned with your core spiritual values; essentially a commitment to what you believe is true.

When it comes to honesty or telling the truth, one often see two different approaches. There's a school of thought that suggests that a good feeling should permeate the truth, regardless of the good or bad news. My mother, on the other hand, can be brutally honest. For instance, one day we were at my parents' house and my mother received a flower arrangement by delivery. When she unwrapped the flowers she saw that three blooms were broken. She called the florist and had them replace the arrangement. Others would have simply accepted that three blooms were broken and thanked the sender. My mother responded to her, saying, "Someone paid good money to send this flower arrangement. I want them to get what they paid for."

You always know where you stand with an honest person. At the same time, you may find that you experience more open conflict with an honest person. Conflict is the engine of all relationships, so honest conflict can only further your relationships. Lies by omission can feel like they're not so bad, but these failures to tell the truth when it's needed can be as damaging or more damaging than a spoken lie. When people hear me speak, I want them to tell me if I missed the mark. That is the only way that I know to grow and do a better job. I don't always expect agreement, but I do expect candor.

I want to challenge you to take the risk of being un- popular when the truth needs to be told. This book is about relationships, not popularity. Honesty is freedom for you and those around you. It is freedom to grow and develop as human beings and to grow and develop your business.

Going Within:

Investment Advice

After we started our firm on October 1, 1995. I knew that relationships were important so I started a networking campaign in San Antonio to meet people and become better known. It's not what you know or who you know, it's *who knows you*. I had to become better known in our community, so I began attending social events, chamber events; all kinds of events. I adhered to Jeffery Gitomer's *Fifty-Butt Rule*: if there were fifty butts in a room, mine was one of them. I carefully thought about my goals and then went looking for someone who could help me accomplish them.

Are you picking up on a theme here? It was all about me! ME, ME, ME!!! I was looking for our next victim. My four words of self-talk were *Who can help me*? If I saw a person in a suit, I'd start a conversation. I just looked for prosperous business professionals. It was a narrow and shortsighted way to network ...and selfish. Did I mention selfish? I was being selfish and that was the attitude that I conveyed. Despite all of my work, I was being unattractive to the people around me.

Naturally, I did not build strong positive relationships. After awhile, I realized from my lack of success that I was just posing. Ouch! My self-esteem took a hit. I had to be honest with myself. I looked in the mirror and said, "I'm a hypocrite and a poseur if I can't do a better job of networking. After several months, I was getting less and less confident about building a business based on networking.

One day it hit me: I was one word off in my self-talk, and I changed one word. Suddenly, instead of asking, Who can help me? I began asking, *Who can I help?* I surmise that if I can help enough people get what they want, chances are that I'll get what I want. After all, one of the best, Zig Ziglar--rest his soul-- said as much himself.

I became consumed with helping people get what they wanted. Sometimes I would call a banker or perhaps I would float a resume or send someone contact information. I was always on the lookout to find ways that I could help other people. That's where my success actually began. I began receiving referrals, benefits and rewards that were too numerous to count. All along, I helped others without any expectation of a return favor. In fact, some of my benefits just came to me independently because I had just made myself more attractive to the world.

In order for me to be happy, in order for me to be successful in sales and in life, I had to be honest with myself. I had to admit that I was a self-centered person that was going nowhere, fast. Then, I had to begin giving from my heart. That is the only way that leads to ever expanding success. When I changed my strategy from being an interesting person to an interested one, I began to attract business and benefits like manna from heaven. I still struggle with my selfish tendencies. To this day, I am truly a work-in-progress.

Reaching Out:

Train Wreck Jack

When you're in a relationship with someone, anyone really, there are two general areas of conversation: your relationship and everything else. Some people go through life without having many conversations that are actually about their relationships. Being able to bring up the relationship and discuss it without being emotionally charged around it is important to the life of the relationship. When it comes to honesty with other people, the two most tempting forms of dishonesty are lies of omission and the failure to speak about the problem in the relationship. Eventually, one of these two things will end the relationship.

I have seen partnerships dissolved when parties realized that they haven't been honest with each other. You may see one of your business relationships end because of some level of dishonesty but you move on and develop other relationships and you think to yourself, "That's behind me." Wrong! When you leave a relationship because of honesty issues, that experience is your constant companion in one way or another. It's out there: bad will. Your community absorbs it and sends it back to you. When you most need to establish trust with a potential client or partner, your past will come bubbling up. As kids we used to say, "Lies can't hide."

Many people don't want to rock the boat, they don't like to feel uncomfortable, and so they aren't being honest with each other or with themselves. Many of us are settling for a mediocre relationship because we don't want to take the risk of open conflict. Ultimately, we could end up losing everything. Making no decision is in reality often the worst decision. You may wonder how I came about my wisdom on this subject. I came about it the hard way.

The year 2000 found me in business with a young man named Clint Swindall. Clint was younger than I and I had acted as a kind of mentor to him as we built a sales consulting practice together. Eventually, Clint wanted to separate and begin working for himself as a professional speaker. We agreed that I would buy him out in the summer of that year.

Early in the year, I suspected that the world was moving to more Web-based training from traditional classroom training. I saw successful companies offering E-learning, Web-based learning. I thought maybe I should try to align my company with a company that does Web- based training. I noticed an article in the San Antonio Business Journal featuring a company called Bold Minds. A man named Kirk Caddell was principal of this company outlined in the business journal as the future of training. I approached him and decided that we should talk about combining our resources. We started talking and the more we talked, the better the idea of merger sounded.

The first mistake I made was not being honest with my partner, Clint Swindall, at the time. I did not mention to him that I was involved in these merger discussions with Bold Minds. Clint and I had an agreement that we would both work part-time in the business and on other projects, so we split ownership and went out to find our own projects. His projects had to do with becoming a recognized keynote speaker and my projects centered on training.

I was greedy. I wanted to keep the deal from Clint so that I didn't have to split the profits with him when I bought him out. So, I chose not to tell him. I began secret talks with Bold Minds, framing a joint venture, a joining of equals. I would be the CEO and Kirk would be the president. Bold Minds and NextStep Solutions would merge. As we were progressing in our talks, I kept it quiet.

In August, just before Labor Day, I bought out Clint. At the end of our toast at The Cigar Club in San Antonio, we hoisted our beer toasting the transfer of ownership. As Clint signed the stock agreements over to me and I signed the check, Clint was happy and I was happy. I was especially happy that he didn't have a clue what was going on with Bold Minds. I thought I had gotten away with something.

In October, I went up to the board of Bold Minds and presented a plan for a merger of NextStep Solutions and Bold Minds. At the beginning of the year 2000, dot com stocks were going through the roof. By the second quarter, the tide was changing for Internet firms. Bold Minds was an Internet company and the Board of Directors began to see the dot com bubble burst. The board had felt much more comfortable with the merger idea in February than they did in October.

In principle, our two firms acted as if we had already merged, but no actual agreement had been signed. Kirk and I proceeded with our new business plan. We started merging customers and blending offices. I moved my office to the Fine Silver building in down- town San Antonio on October first. We blended staffs and customers then planned to blend stock options at year's end.

Around the first of November, Kirk and I had an appointment to talk to a major client in Las Vegas. This client was a multinational marketing company. I was excited about the deal and anxious to proceed but I got to the airport and Kirk was nowhere to be found.

I tried to call Kirk, but I couldn't get him. Time passed. I arrived in Las Vegas and began my meeting with the client: still no Kirk. Finally, I called Kirk's wife's cell phone, only to learn from her that he was at the office! Little did I know that Kirk did not tell me that the board voted against the merger of our companies. Kirk didn't tell me Thursday night before I flew out Friday. He waited until I was in Las Vegas looking bad and he still didn't have the nerve to tell me.

This vote by the board of Bold Minds was a devastating turn of events for my solely owned company. I had invested thousands of dollars and hours at the very time when Kirk and the Bold Minds board were having second thoughts.

I consulted my attorney and he told me that I had a legitimate lawsuit but that I wouldn't have a friend left in town. Besides, he added, it would take years to collect the money.

I was dishonest by omission with my partner, Clint, by not telling him the truth about my meetings with Bold Minds. Kirk was dishonest with me by omission. I reaped what I had sowed and I learned the honesty lesson in stereo. I chose not to proceed with the lawsuit.

The Next Step

Sales is a career that is fraught with subtle opportunities to be dishonest (Old salesmen joke: do you know how to tell if a Sales rep is lying? Their lips are moving). It is a frequent complaint among customers that it was very easy for them to get into a deal and very difficult for them to get out. If your customers trust you, they will think that you are honest and they will take your advice. I suggest that you do not abuse this trust.

Often, I hear of clients saying, "I could have dealt with that if you would have just told me." You never get a *second* chance to make a *first* impression. Act as if every encounter is either a first or a last encounter with that client.

Do you have a document that explains in clear English what dependencies are involved in making a deal with you? Does this document also explain how the client can exit the deal? If you don't have this document, have one written that is short, easy to read and in print that is at least twelve point.

With this in hand, make it a practice at every contract signing to give the document to your client and to read it out loud with them.

Did this exercise cause you to make some changes in your life? If so, I'd like to hear about it. Send me an e-mail telling me what happened at jack@lifesasalescall.com.

Building Block of Successful Sales

When you open a new relationship, that client gets a new Ambassador: YOU! What is more, that firm becomes an integral component of your N.E.E.R. Strategy--*Network of Existing Economic Relationships*. Said another way, by mutual decree, you can open doors for each other, provide warm introductions, and refer business back and forth--without the burdened overhead of another Sales rep. Think about it: doesn't N.E.E.R. beat F.A.R. (*Firing At Random*) any day of the week? Absolutely!

Aside from the value they receive for their investment in you, nothing endears a client to you more, than your enthusiastic testimonials about their business. "Testimonials?" you say. "That would mean that I was their client or customer". Exactly.

Become your client's crusader. Obviously, this isn't always possible, but when it is, do it and then rave about their service or product to the people in your network. Today's Social Media options facilitate this process. Between Twitter, Facebook, Linkedin or a myriad of other options it is possible to become your client's crusader, and sharing the success of their business such as marketing training, knowledge of new markets and contacts. Whatever your expertise, ask yourself, "How can our skills assist my client in growing their business?"

Gather the brochures and market literature on your client's products as well as a number of their business cards. Ask them to email you PDFs of their product/service sheets, for you to save and forward. Display these and hand them out to the people that you meet and know each day. Be sure to check with them to discover any new products or services they might be offering. Your open willingness to help your client will be received with deep appreciation.

Referrals are the lifeblood of most companies, just as they are for you. As you give, you shall receive. Make it your goal to send your client at least one referral a month. This may not always work out, but if you set your intention on this goal, you will ultimately send your client business.

You may have the opportunity to buy public stock in your client's company. Some clients respond warmly when you extend your hand of friendship by taking them to a game, to a show or to hear a popular speaker pertinent to their field. It takes creative initiative to be in a relationship. You have to think of varied and unique ways of building bridges between you and them. It better feel like more than just work to you. At this point, I am going to assume that you have found a way to mirror affinity to your client and that you genuinely like them and they like you. As you deepen your relationship with them, you are actually enriching your life and having fun.

What if you are a woman and your client is a man or vice versa? This goes back to your integrity and your communication skills. Include spouses. If there is not a spouse on one side or the other, be professional and continue to maintain and deepen your relationship. The more that we can create community regardless of marital status, race, religion or gender the more successful we will be in business and in life. Studies show that diversity in business groups increase profits. It's harder to create and maintain a diversity program, but the efforts pay dividends. Did I mention increased profits? I say this because as much as we all pay lip service to creating affinity with individuals and groups that are not our own, many of us find that we really don't ever stray too far from our comfort zone.

You know that a comfort zone is made of Silly Putty (I'm dating myself again) don't you? It's as pliable and as open to new cultures and personalities as you are. Get comfortable with being uncomfortable for a period of time. Your discomfort will quickly pass. Be secure in yourself enough to invest yourself in knowing and being with people who are very different from you or whose lifestyles are some trouble for you to accommodate. Put yourself out in order to get to know someone else. Give first and get second! When you do this, you open up new markets, you become a role model and you deepen and grow your relationship with yourself: the source of your success.

Jack's Snack:

"The best teacher is one whose life is the text".

Chapter 13

Integrity

Integrity, for me, is like the key in which a song is played. It is staying true to the path you have chosen from the beginning to the end, through all of the ups and downs and tricky arpeggios. To what values are you committed? If you don't have these clearly set out in your mind, then now would be a good time to write them down. I am committed, for instance, to maintaining a balanced life that includes a spiritual aspect to it. As a result, I try to maintain a regular spiritual routine. Though not always convenient, I find that making time to read, pray and attend services is downright painful at times and that's just the tip of the iceberg! Maintaining a spiritual practice means that I have to be clear with myself about exactly who I am going to be in the world. That's a lot more effort than just sliding along and reacting to what I like and dislike.

For you, integrity may look like a certain diet and exercise schedule. It may mean that you attend a twelve-step program, say no when you mean no or admit that you are wrong to your boss, your spouse or your child. Integrity looks different to each person because each person has his or her own set of values. At the end of the day, you find yourself living your life, based on a compass, not a clock, and you always strive for True North on your journey.

We like to surround ourselves with people who share some of our values such as honesty, fidelity or hard work. Nevertheless, we may find that not everyone places a high value on helping disadvantaged kids or protecting the water quality.

Decide what you stand for and stand for it. Integrity is who you are when nobody's looking.

Going Within:

Speaking from the Heart

I have to tell you that when I came to write this chapter, I was tempted to write about an incident where I did something that followed through on my values--an interesting little story of some kind. The more I thought about the subject of integrity, however, the more I realized that I have an ongoing struggle to stay true to my values and it's a struggle that I don't like to talk about. So, here it is. I do not feel comfortable talking about my feelings. After almost four decades of being in business, three sons, a second marriage and lots of acquaintances and few friendships, I've figured at least one thing out: the quality and depth of my relationships is directly related to my ability to express feelings.

When I can look my millennial sons in the eyes and tell them, I'm scared. I love you and watching you make bad decisions scares me. What if you get hurt? That would break my heart. My sons are very clear on what motivates me, on how I feel about them and on how their actions would affect me. If I say to my son, as I have done in the past, "No. That's the end of the story. No." Well, then, I've done a good job as a parent in setting boundaries and working to keep my child safe but I have not deepened my relationship with that adult child, as they turn 25, 27 and 29 years old, in the Fall of 2015.

When I say to a client, "I'm happy to hear from you. I thought about you the other day. Your loss hit home with me and made me appreciate what I have." That client knows that I have empathy and compassion for them. They know that I am capable of thoughtfully considering them and reflecting on my own life. On the other hand, if I say, as I have often done, "Good to hear from you! How are you?" I communicate a passing interest that may or may not be particularly thought-out or personal.

When I listen to a new client tell me how their first two businesses failed, I can say, "That's tough." Or I can admit to them that I too have had to let go of enterprises and that I hoped to "fail forward and fail fast" while learning something from the experience. The pain of having to radically redirect a dream can be devastating, yet doing it can make the next attempt successful. As you can see, talking about my feelings, changes my conversations and my relationships, from casual, shallow experiences to real, human connections. I coined a new word last year: *nonversation.* That's a noun to describe a conversation where nothing of substance is ever said. A superficial exchange of words is an understatement. You've heard them before.

Marriage is that layer of integrity that is closest to my core relationship with myself. In marriage, my willingness to say, "I'm afraid you will..."or "I feel like..." can spell the difference between a happy union and an uneasy alliance. Do I even need to tell you how my ability to say, "I saw you walking in the parking lot at the drug store today and realized how beautiful you are all over again," can create an environment of romance and appreciation? You know what I'm talking about!

Every day, every hour, every minute I'm uncomfortable being emotionally expressive and vulnerable. I struggle because I have a value system that places human connections as a high priority.

139

I struggle because I have made a commitment to being all that I can be and that means revealing myself to others. I was raised, like many men, to be "manly" and tough. As I've matured in my career and my relationships, I learned that being a man means being strong enough to show my feelings.

Stoicism is a common trait of many women as well. We all have different degrees of ease around expressing our emotions. If you are committed to relationship sales then you're going to have to take a long look at how you talk about your feelings with others. This practice of personal integrity may not be the most exciting story to tell but it is the most effective way to reach out and touch someone else. Touching people: that's life and that's sales.

Reaching Out:

"Built with integrity. Backed by service". Do you remember that marketing slogan, probably dating back to the sixties or seventies? The name of the company that used it (Motorola?) escapes me at this moment, but integrity is front and center. Unfortunately, integrity is better shown than told. Integrity is who we are, when nobody's looking.

Bill Morrow is the Founder and former CEO of Grande Communications, a U.S. telecommunications form, based in San Marcos, TX. The company was established in 1999, when it was the recipient of the largest round of venture capital funding in Texas, at the time. One does not attract investors like that, without having a stellar reputation of integrity--among other things. Who is Bill Morrow when nobody's looking? Our story takes us to an HEB (a privately-owned grocery store chain in TX, that is now the 8th largest in the country) parking lot in San Marcos, a 'burb a few miles south of Austin. Bill finishes loading up his SUV with a heaping shopping cart of groceries. He's parked in the far parking lot perimeter, and is now seen walking his empty cart back to one of the repositories near the entrance of the store, of course.

Who sees him? One of the ladies from his back office, is waiting to see what Bill does, from her car in the same lot. "Sue" was impressed that a busy CEO type like Bill Morrow, took the time to walk his empty grocery cart back to the rack, instead of leaving it stranded in a very busy parking lot, only to roll into a car or two. Later in the week, she strolled by his office, just to tell him how impressed she was with his gesture. Bill is the same person, even when nobody is looking--or so he thought!

The Next Step

If you would like to receive great referrals from your clients, you have to be the kind of person to whom they would want to refer their colleagues and friends. Earlier in my writing, I shared what I call the Four Laws of Referability. Read through these and check off those that apply to you. Those that don't apply to you are a red flag that you may not be the kind of person to your client, that you want your client to be to you.

- Do you selflessly promote your client's business?

- Are you providing quality referrals to your client's business on a regular basis? If yes, how many in a month?

- Do you carry your clients' literature and / or business cards, and hand them out when applicable?

- Do you work to keep your clients informed of news you hear about new developments or changes in their industry?

- Are you a client of your client? There is no better way to prove the depth of your relationship than by participating in a quid pro quo exchange.

- Do you routinely finish what you start?

- When you say that you are going to do something, do you do it?

- Are you consistently on time?

- Do you show consideration and respect by always saying "Please" and "Thank you?"

When you maintain an attitude of service and servitude, you are being the kind of person you are asking your client to be when they send you referrals. This is integrity.

How is this working for you? Send me and e-mail and tell me. I want to know! jack@lifesasalescall.com.

Building Blocks of Successful Sales

If you have listened, responded and basically created and maintained a relationship with someone, then in order for you to remain consistent to your values, keep this idea in mind, "Serve first, sell second". People buy things from friends more than they do from sales professionals. There's no need to sweat a sale or be pushy. Just be yourself and remember to serve first and sell second. BNI International states that Givers Gain. This maintains relationship integrity on every level.

I'm fond of sharing a Zig Ziglarism, that people don't care how much you know until they know how much you care. As interesting as it is to learn how the ancient Egyptians made ceramic tiles before they came to Italy, that information is not going to build rapport with me. On the other hand, if you were to ask me about the origin of my passion for sports or how I got into sales training, I might get the impression that you care. I will remember your curiousity.

When you do speak, speak from your heart. Human beings respond to strongly held convictions. I bought a giant chocolate bar the other day from a young man who knocked on my door. I don't need to eat a chocolate bar the size of a toaster, but I was convinced that I should buy the bar because of the young man's own conviction that it was for a good cause. He didn't know squat about chocolate, but hey, he felt strongly that selling this bar to me was an important, worthwhile and beneficial way to invest his time. I responded positively to his deep convictions.

Your integrity starts with how kind and honest you are with yourself. It expands outward to the tools and behaviors that you use to create sales. Speak from your heart and you will get an answer every time.

Jack's Snack:

"Words are words. Explanations are explanations. Promises are promises, but only RESULTS are reality".

Chapter 14

Persistent

In the world of sales and business you must persist. I teach The Rule of Fifteen. The rule states that if, over time, you can find a way to ask for a client's business fifteen times or more, you have an eighty percent chance of at least getting a small, "Yes!"More than half of all sales reps give up trying to get the sale after the first rejection. The Rule of Fifteen rewards the persistent sales person. Ask someone for his or her business. If you can persist and find a way to do that sincerely, they will respond. So many people quit asking when they are one "no" away from being awarded the sale. Allow me to repeat from earlier: If you don't A.S.K. you don't G.E.T. Be sure that you are constantly asking questions. Or, in the world of commission based sales: If you don't A.S.K., you don't E.A.T. Never give up. Make that extra call. Plan one last sales call before you fold your tent for the day.

Going Within:

More Than Talk

The year was 1981 and I worked for Big Blue, IBM. It was my second year of being on a sales quota - my second year in the territory. When the President of IBM, GSD Division, Lew Gray came to St. Louis and visited our branch office, I was a rookie, barely shaving, and looking all of twenty-three years old. When he had finished speaking, he asked if there were any questions. I raised my hand from the back of the room. "I have a question," I said, "How do I get your job?" Ballsy? You bet! It was a way for me to stand out and be noticed, albeit a risky one.

Of the one hundred and forty people in that room, he approached me at the end of the meeting.

He told me that I had to do things better than anyone else does. He said, "John (my real name), be the best at whatever you decide to do."

What can I say? The man inspired me. At that moment, I looked him in the eyes and said, "I plan to lead the country in new account sales this year. My goal this year is to sell at least one computer a week." (This was a year before the advent of the PC!)

Lew looked at me incredulously, "Do you know how many sales reps there are in the country? There are four thousand! That's a pretty bold prediction."

I held my ground. I said, "I think I'm up to the task. I won't give up."Famous last words! In fact, that year was the most incredible year of my life. Everyone from the President of IBM/GSD on down knew my goal: to lead the country in new account sales. Once I made the goal clear, I had to go execute it.

I started out pretty well; I was selling a few computers. IBM corporate offices noticed my progress and started sending people out to help me. They wanted to help me achieve my goals in the business. Whenever I knew that a sales pro was coming down to my office, I would stack my day to make it the most incredible business day in this person's life. I would have to do some unnatural things to prepare so that they could report back that I was a wonder kid. For instance, I had a remote territory and had to drive ninety miles to make my first sales call. I would pick the person up at the hotel at five a.m. because we'd have a breakfast meeting with a potential IBM customer. We'd drive to a greasy spoon in Illinois and from there we would have a series of qualified calls with someone who was about to buy a computer. I choreographed it like the director of a play. Usually, we would get back around eight or nine o'clock at night.

"If this guy works this hard," I wanted them to think, "No wonder he's successful." My sales picked up. I was near the top but not at the top. There I was, twenty-three years old and competing with people who had been in business all of their life. The more I sold, the more support I got! I opened a new account every week all year: fifty-three accounts, one per week.

Every day I worked a twelve-hour day. I wouldn't take no for an answer, at least, not until I heard the word fifteen times. I was so confident in my ability to sell, that I'd go to our St. Louis warehouse and pack a new computer and put it in the car and find someone to sell it to. I was the guy who got in a rowboat, brought tartar sauce and went out to meet Moby Dick every day.

The top sellers at IBM receive The Eagle Award with an automatic Golden Circle qualification. If I made the Golden Circle, IBM would send me to Hawaii with my future wife. Since I was getting married the next year, this was good timing. In addition, I would receive ten thousand dollars in cash and a valuable piece of art. So, there I was, cruisin' on, cruisin' on. IBM was darkening the sky with people to help me in my pursuit.

Only one night that year do I recall having trouble sleeping. It was the next to the last day and I realized that I was going to have to sell five computers in two days to meet my goal of selling fifty-two computers a year. I thought there was no way on God's earth that I could sell five computers. So, on the last day of the year, I showed up at work at six o'clock in the morning as usual. I opened the door to the office and there stood at least twenty people! The whole office showed up to help me. Sales reps, systems engineers, administrators and managers, all surprised me and offered to help because they knew what was at stake. They all banded together to help me sell the five computers.

At the end of the day, we had sold six computers! I at last led the world in new account sales at IBM. Lew Gray came in and presented me a suitcase with ten thousand dollars in cash and I gave half of it away to those who had helped me. The money was not important. What was important was achieving the goal. That was one of those crowning turning points in my life.

Persistence in achieving goals is the number one thing that you can bring to the table.

Reaching Out:

He Wanted to Play Ball

When I first moved to St. Louis one of my first purchases was a duplex. This meant that I shared a wall with another family. Living next door to me was a young couple with a small son named Billy. I was young and single and out of school and Billy was eleven years old.

Both of Billy's parents worked. After school, Billy liked to throw a baseball and he would ask me to play catch.

Billy only wanted to do one thing -play baseball. No matter how many people he had to ask, or how many times he had to ask, he would persist until someone played baseball with him.

As long as he was a kid and people asked him what he wanted to be when he grew up, Billy always said the same thing, "I want to be a professional baseball player.' Adults are usually amused when they hear a grand dream like that. They think, "Oh, all little boys want to be baseball players."

During the three or four years that I lived next door to Billy, he never stopped throwing a baseball. I moved out of the townhouse when he started high school.

Every year Billy persisted until he became the best baseball player he could be. Fast-forward to 1996 and Bill Mueller signed his first baseball contract with the San Francisco Giants in the minor leagues.

Here is what the "Billy page" (http:/www.geocities.com/citygirl32.geo/billmueller2.html) on the Internet says about Bill, "Every chance he got, he played hard, giving no less than 100%. He quietly showed Giants fans and the rest of the world that he could be an important player in the team's future, if given a chance. He put up consistent numbers at the plate while making spectacular plays in the field.

"Bill made such an impact on the Giants management that he was back with the team the next season. The trade of popular third baseman Matt Williams made it hard for fans to accept that Bill could somehow take over the day-to-day grind at third. Mark Lewis was brought in by the Giants to platoon at third base with Bill but when he got hurt in the beginning of the season, Bill made the best of the opportunity that he was given. He played well, both on the field and at the plate. Each day that went by, he became more and more vital to the team's success. Bill was no longer just the guy playing third; he became someone his teammates constantly relied on - whether it was to get on base, deliver a much-needed clutch hit, or make a spectacular play to help his pitcher out of a jam. He was consistent in his efforts throughout the season and there is no doubt in anyone's mind that he was one of the many people who played an important part in helping the Giants win the NLWest division title.

"During the months preceding the 1998 season, the Giants, recognizing Bill's talents, concentrated on making sure he would be a part of the team for years to come. And when all was said and done, Bill was signed to a three-year contract."

Bill joined the Chicago Cubs after leaving San Francisco and later played third base for the World Champion Boston Red Sox, after winning a batting title. What a journey, indeed!

The Next Step

Do you have a goal in mind that is big and challenging? Have you told someone else about it? How many other people have you enrolled in helping you to achieve your goal?

What do you have to do to achieve this goal? What will you do if that doesn't work? What will you do if that doesn't work? How persistent are you willing to be?

I want to know! Send me an e-mail jack@lifesasalescall.com and tell me about your goals. Let me know what your plan is for today, tomorrow and however long it takes for you to achieve that goal.

Building Blocks of Successful Sales

That great American writer, Ralph Waldo Emerson equated a heroic person with a persistent person. He said, "The characteristic of heroism is its persistency. All men have wandering impulses, fits and starts of generosity. But when you have chosen your part, abide by it, and do not weakly try to reconcile yourself with the world. The heroic cannot be the common, not the common the heroic." These are old-fashioned words, yet I think Emerson's idea that a hero is that person who sets their mind upon a prize or goal and remains focused on that goal, excluding all distractions and influences that may dissuade him or her from their goal. In the world of business the only winners are those who have failed many times and yet persist.

When we hear the word hero, we think of someone who is powerful in some way. Persistence is power. It is the power of focus over ego and faith over discouragement. The miracle of life is that you just never know what's going to happen. You may think you know what the parameters are in a situation, but you don't. So, don't give up. Don't give up! The possibilities are endless.

Two ways to jumpstart your career when you feel like throwing in the towel are exhibiting a sense of humor and uniqueness. Life's a journey, not a destination so enjoy the trip. Keep the word play in your mind all of the time. Play is fun, play is what we pay to do, play is why we "work." Let's change that to, "Work is play." Lighten up and laugh. Make your workday a game and enroll other people in playing with you. When you experience a setback remember, it's only a game. In other words, this is serious fun and you can always try again, play a different way or take a break and start over. The important thing in relationships, life and sales is to have fun and communicate that attitude to the people around you. Not only will they buy what you have to sell, they will buy you. That is a great experience to have.

One way to make the game interesting is to figure out what makes you completely different from the next guy. For instance, if the thing that makes your Italian tiles better than the other guy's Italian tiles is the intricate designs, then by all means have some T- shirts or silk scarves printed with some of these designs and give them away. Do something eye-catching and fun. If the tiles are sturdier, learn karate and give a demonstration of their un-breakability for your clients. They will love the show! Whatever you have to offer, make sure that it is unique and valuable and then have fun with that.

Life's a sales call and sales calls are life. I'm here to tell you that it's a fascinating and often uncomfortable journey. To be truly successful in life and relationships, I've had to cultivate the ability to be comfortable with discomfort...for awhile. Whether it's creating affinity and likeability, being honest, trusting or persistent, I know it's going to cause me some pain if I do it with integrity. That's o.k. because the rewards of creating and maintaining relationships with other people are infinite. The practice of relationship sales expands my life out into ever widening spheres. Schmoozing makes me money but only in a narrow and short corridor.

I invite you today to treat yourself with great respect and then take that relationship and replicate it in your personal and business worlds. Let me know how it goes, I wish you all the success in the world in your sales call known as life!

ABOUT THE AUTHOR

Jack is the CEO and founder of **NextStep Solutions** (NSS), Sales specialists headquartered in Houston, TX. **NextStep Solutions**, www.nextstep-solutions.com, is known, worldwide, for increasing client sales, through a *customerized* approach to *strategy, training, coaching, and consulting* services. **NextStep Solutions**—founded in 1995—inspires sales greatness, focusing on building relationships and enhancing communications skills, delivering quantifiable results.

In 2005, Jack came to Houston, to become a radio personality, hosting a daily, live business talk show, *"Where Wall Street Meets Main Street"*, heard during morning drive-time, across the State of Texas, on **The BizRadio Network**—and on the internet around the world.

After graduating from the University of Illinois, Champaign-Urbana in 1978, Jack began a decade-long career with IBM. He quickly established a stellar reputation as the best "new account" Sales professional in the company, leading the nation in new accounts opened—53 systems in 52 weeks—BEFORE the advent of the PC! The most amazing part: *he did it in his SECOND year on quota.* Upon being awarded the highest IBM Sales award—*The Eagle*—his professional speaking career was inadvertently launched, when he traveled across the country, sharing his Sales techniques with hundreds of other IBM professionals.

Jack wrote the book on sales. In fact, he's the author of the bestselling book, *"**Life's A Sales Call: How To Succeed In The World's Oldest Profession**"*, on sale everywhere and at www.amazon.com. He now travels the world, speaking before thousands of people, delivering presentations with extremely high content in an entertaining and inspirational fashion, in areas of *Sales, Marketing, Service and Leadership*.

Jack is very involved in the local community. He founded and capitalized *The Barnabas Society*, www.barnabassociety.org, a 501 c 3 corporation, that raises and distributes money and resources to people in their greatest times of need, with all the funds donated anonymously.

Jack and his wife Kemi Kim, live in Fulshear Texas where they are enjoying suburban life.

Jack's Seminars

Life's A Sales Call - Everyone in your firm can be an effective "business Ambassador" by enhancing communication and relationship skills.

In Life, K.A.S.H. Is King - Cash maybe king, but K.A.S.H. is where the real equity is. Your team will begin to know their knowledge, amplify their attitudes, strengthen their skills and hone their habits.

Discover Your Next Sale - Your sales team will learn why the selling process must needs by questioning and listening.

Scoring From the Red Zone - Open more relationships and accounts by converting stalls to objections and overcoming them, early and effectively - once and for all.

Leadership Lessons - Learn the difference between being a leader and a boss and how to inspire positive changes in the behavior of employees.

Balance On Life's Superhighway - To success in life, we must balance all areas, including professional, personal, psychological, physical and spiritual needs. Learn how and why.

A Case for S.M.A.R.T. Goals - Become one of the prosperous minority who conceive S.M.A.R.T. goals - achieve them regularly. Learn the 5-step process that will change your life.

The Networking Game - Networking is working. It is the prospecting tool for the next millennium. Your group will learn how to quickly qualify candidates and have fun doing it.

For further information or to book a seminar with

NextStep Solutions, Inc.

info @nextstep-solutions.com

Jack's Training Curricula

Mastering Professional Sales (MPS)

Mastering Professional Sales provides the tools and the training to make the shift from transactional selling to the Relationship Selling Process®. Each two to three hour session enables participants to focus on Matching your company's Unique Value Proposition with your customer's Dominant Buying Motives.

Mastering Professional Leadership (MPL)

Each module represents a two to three=hour Leadership Development Training Session for a target audience comprised of up to twenty participants. Some of the module are stand-alone sessions, in that they provide a dynamic learning opportunity for a luncheon engagement or as in insert to enhance a company retreat. Many of the sessions are most beneficial when paired with other modules.

Mastering Customer Service (MCS)

Mastering Customer Service provides he attitudes, behavior and communication skills to assist any professional in a service capacity. Each two-to-three-hour session assists in the handling of both "internal" and "external" customers.

Thank you for your order!

NextStep Solutions, Inc.

5090 Richmond Ave. Suite 400

Houston, TX 77056

Email: info@nextstep-solutions.com